Robina Lambert

DOLMENS

AND

DUENDE

*with best
wishes

Robina*

Rudling House

Rudling House Publishing Limited
Suite 11480 145-157 St John Street
London EC1V 4PY

The right of Robina Lambert to be identified
as the author of this work has been asserted
by her in accordance with the
Copyright, Designs and Patents Act, 1988

Published in the UK in 2012 by Rudling House
A CIP catalogue record for this book is
available from the British Library

Font: Dante MT 11.5 pt
ISBN 978-0-9562760-8-7
© 2012 Robina Lambert
Cover design: Ole Dammegård
Original artwork: Helen O'Leary
Colour and b/w photographs: Robina Lambert

Printed and bound by CPI Group (UK) Ltd, Croydon, CR0 4YY

DEDICATION

This book is dedicated to Helen Moore, a life-long friend. In May 2009, at the age of 95, she visited Andalucía for the first time. Her enthusiasm to experience as much as possible during her short stay here and the lively interest she showed in the people and the culture of the region encouraged me to finish it.

ACKNOWLEDGEMENTS

The author would like to thank Helen O'Leary for her invaluable assistance and Peter Brookes for his encouragement. Without them this book would not have been written, completed, or published.

DOLMENS AND DUENDE

Exploring the culture
of
Andalucía

THE PAST

IS ALWAYS PRESENT

BEFORE US

ABOUT THE AUTHOR

The author has lived in Andalucía since 1987. Inspired in her late teens by a language teacher devoted to Spain, its music and its customs, she studied Spanish then worked as a translator in London. When she moved to southern Spain, she immediately felt this was where she belonged. Settling permanently in Estepona and integrating happily with the local population, she continues to work as a legal translator and also writes articles and books about the culture and natural environment of Andalucía.

Dolmens and Duende is infused with the author's understanding of and affection for the region she has made her home. The book is not intended as a travel guide but rather a textual companion, something to dip into to deepen a particular experience or to provide a context for the rich cultural mix that is Andalucía.

JAÉN

GRANADA

MÁLAGA   ALMERÍA

NOTES

Names of places have been kept in the original
Spanish, with accents, to avoid any confusion.

All measurements are metric unless otherwise
explained (viz. the Roman 'mile').

DOLMENS AND DUENDE
Exploring the culture of Andalucía

FOREWORD

Wherever you are in the world, culture encompasses everything about society from its beginnings to the present day. Reflecting the hopes, fears and beliefs rooted within our ancestry, at any one time it is a fusion of past and present, the old and the new.

Culture does not only include entertainment, as found in theatre and literature, music and dance, or visits to museums and art galleries. It goes much deeper. It is an expression of the background and contemporary mores of different races or groups of people, an identifying force that survives from generation to generation.

Throughout the ages the area of southern Spain that is now Andalucía has formed a cultural bridge between all points of the compass. The Phoenicians and the Romans arrived from the east bringing their expertise in trade and road building. Also from the east came the Umayyads at the beginning of the 8th century and in their caliphate of Córdoba Hispano-Arab culture thrived for many centuries. The Almoravids and the Almohads travelled from the Sahara and the Magreb, establishing their empire during the 11th to 13th centuries in the region they called Al-Andalus. They all left behind an extraordinary legacy, part of the subsequent intellectual flowering that formed inspiration for the renaissance of art and architecture spreading throughout Europe from Italy and France.

Andalucía has seen a great mixing and a merging of customs and traditions and all have left their mark. Today, with even greater global convergence, it continues to absorb the ethnicity of other societies. This can be seen especially in flamenco which now has overtones of North American jazz, South American tango and Central American salsa, as well as underlying African rhythms. Also in architecture the new and the old combine. One outstanding example is the Málaga Picasso Museum which provides an ancient setting for modern art.

Granada's Alhambra Palace, the Giralda Tower in Sevilla or Grand Mosque in Córdoba are three of the principal sites of cultural interest in the region. But each of the eight provincial capital cities in Andalucía has numerous historic buildings dating from many different eras. There are a great many museums, large and small, dedicated not only to fine and decorative arts, but also to anthropology or palaeontology, dolls, bandits, music or olives, water or wine.

Almost every town and village in the region boasts an ancient castle, cathedral, fortress or monastery. And there are magnificent archaeological sites: the Roman city of Itálica, near Sevilla, and the Bronze Age settlement of Los Millares, near Almería, are two of the most extensive. Many others are little known and seldom visited, others remain to be discovered.

The golden cities of Úbeda and Baeza, on UNESCO's list of World Heritage sites since 2003, are the embodiment of Renaissance art and architecture. But fine examples exist elsewhere in Andalucía. Málaga, Jaén and Sevilla have imposing cathedrals, Cádiz and Granada boast impressive 15th and 16th century buildings and in the provinces of Córdoba, Huelva and Almería there are many large town houses and country mansions built in the 17th and 18th centuries that were once the palatial homes of dukes and counts.

Culture also includes the customs of everyday life that have been practised for centuries. Every area in Andalucía has its own traditions, from the *verdiales* of the Montes de Málaga and folk dances of the Guadalquivir valley, to the grand carnival of Cádiz, horse shows in Jerez de la Frontera and flamenco *tablaos* in Sevilla.

Artisan products are crafted throughout Andalucía, some unique to a particular area, others depicting traditions of past societies. The woollen blankets of Grazalema and the Axarquía are made to designs handed down over centuries. Some of the pottery produced in Úbeda is still fired in ancient Arab kilns using wood pruned from the hundreds of thousands of olive trees growing in the area. Fans and mantillas, rush baskets and wrought iron – even now many of these articles are made completely by hand, using time-honoured methods.

An increasing number and variety of cultural programmes are promoted within Spain and abroad by the Junta de Andalucía, encompassing the whole spectrum of historical customs and traditions of the region. Some take the form of routes across the region. Organised in conjunction with other associations, such as El Legado Andalusí, they trace the architectural and cultural footprints left by the Moors during their eight-century occupancy of Al-Andalus. Others have been devised to follow in the 2000-year-old footsteps of the Romans from Cádiz up the Guadalquivir river valley and through the Subbética area, or to trace those of Bronze Age man in what is now the province of Almería.

Culture is also found in nature. Excursions can be taken to numerous white villages hidden away up spectacular mountain roads or along green river valleys. Others explore the varied landscapes above and below ground, from the dizzy heights of the Sierra Nevada to the depths of wondrous caves. Those at Nerja, where internationally acclaimed dancers, singers and musicians regularly perform, have spectacular stalagmites and stalactites, while in the Cueva de la Pileta near Benaoján, in the Serranía de Ronda, there are some of the most important prehistoric cave paintings in Europe.

Drawing on the wealth of customs and traditions in Andalucía, this book takes you on a journey through the very essence of the region, embracing its people, its history and geography and the rich, complex patchwork of its unique culture. But there is so much that cannot be explained. A dolmen is tangible, it can be seen and touched, but *duende* is something that is felt – it is the magic and the atmosphere, the emotion and the spirit, the very core of the region or its soul.

Not every area of Andalucía is covered or every aspect included, but it is hoped the book will reveal just how much there is to discover in this fascinating region.

CULTURAL FOOTPRINTS

Top of 18th-century watchtower, Cádiz

Dolmen de Menga, near Antequera

Introduction

At first glance it looks as if no human has ever left a footprint in much of the inland areas of Andalucía. On the craggy mountainsides of the sierras, extending south-west to north-east across the region, or on the seemingly endless inland plains, there is little to be seen of past habitation.

New civilisations tended to occupy their predecessors' settlements, but many were eventually abandoned and left to be covered over by the natural movement of the earth. Beneath the surface, evidence of much of the area's history still awaits discovery. But what can be seen today of Andalucía's distant past, dating back to prehistoric times, are cave paintings near Cádiz, Phoenician remains in Málaga and dolmens.

Outside crumbling stone walls enclosing the settlement of a bygone civilisation, dome-shaped hills reveal a necropolis, or burial place, its entrance marked by a dolmen. One enormous megalith rests horizontally upon other slightly smaller ones sunk vertically into the ground in an amazing feat of monumental constructive dexterity. Beyond this portal a narrow passageway leads either to a simple circular tomb or to various chambers, depending upon the size of the burial ground. Stones are balanced upon stones in a beehive shape and the whole construction is often covered with earth to form an artificial tumulus.

Prehistoric man and the subsequent conquerors and invaders needed to travel, to seek food and water, to trade or to plunder. The paths between each new settlement eventually created well trodden routes of communication. Some were mere footpaths, others subsequently wide enough for horse-drawn carts. But one thing all these roads had in common, until the Romans arrived, they were very rough indeed.

Until recently men and their mules used to leave their inland villages in autumn to wend their way along mountain trails over the sierras of Andalucía. They came south seeking 'brown gold' – the fruit of the *algarrobo* or locust tree whose beans, when ripe, are long, hard and dark-brown and contain small, shiny seeds. These seeds, or carats, were originally thought to be identical and were used on precision scales as weights to measure gold.

The bean pods of the *algarrobo* have multiple uses: as a substitute for cocoa in chocolate; an ingredient in confectionery and cosmetics; for medicinal purposes and as fodder for animals. All these men asked for was permission to sleep the night on someone's *finca*, tether their animals and be provided with water. They gathered the beans and, taking fifty per cent for themselves, were on their way leaving no trace of their stay.

Those same mountain routes had been previously travelled by bandits and smugglers. Today some are being re-established as *senderos*, paths for walkers, bicyclists and horse riders, and are linked to others in neighbouring regions or countries. Within Andalucía they form a network, some extending more than 50 kilometres (GR – *Gran Recorrido*) and shorter ones from ten to thirty kilometres (PR – *Pequeño Recorrido*). All are marked and signposted and maps are usually provided by local authorities. They tend wherever possible to avoid made-up roads and often lead to a refuge or a spot of inestimable beauty.

Many of these paths join up with the long European route, the E-4, which begins near Tarifa and ends in Greece. Those who follow them are the present day 'pilgrims'. They do not walk towards a cathedral on a spiritual mission; they are not trading or invading; they are merely seeking tranquillity and the beauty of nature. Out of respect for the natural environment, very few leave their 'footprint'.

Medieval pilgrims travelled great distances. They did so without regard to feudal frontiers or the boundaries of a realm, braving not only inhospitable areas, inclement weather and hazardous terrain, but also brigands, angry locals and wild animals. Wherever possible they used existing tracks, or followed watercourses by way of undulating valleys. Often though, they were forced to strike out on their own through virgin forests and untrodden ravines. Many left their footprint or mark by constructing a refuge along the way to serve as a shelter for others following the route they had established.

According to medieval legend, the Milky Way was formed out of the dust churned up by the hundreds of thousands of pilgrims heading for Santiago de Compostella in north-western Spain. The Camino de Santiago, or Way of St. James, is enjoying a popular revival, but the present-day footprints are becoming a problem. There are too many of them. For a less visited alternative the Vía de la Plata, or Silver Way, is well worth exploring.

Base of Roman milestone, Acinipo, near Ronda

The Silver Way

Silver, or *plata*, is unlikely to have been transported along this ancient trade route in western Iberia. The contemporary name, Vía de la Plata, is thought to have been the result of phonetic confusion by the Christians of the original Roman name of Vía Delapidata, meaning the 'Stone Paved Way'. Also known as the Camino Mozárabe, it was used by the Moors to invade regions beyond Al-Andalus and to spread their culture northwards.

Some original Roman paving is still visible in Andalucía. There are stretches between Benaocaz and Ubrique in the province of Cádiz, and great slabs of precisely hewn stone tumble down towards the Manilva's sulphur baths in the province of Málaga. These roads were an amazing feat of engineering. Wherever possible they ran in a straight line and were made up of layers of different materials which varied according to the geographical location.

Once the trajectory had been plotted and the land excavated down to the bedrock, the road was levelled then covered with small stones to make the *statumen* layer. On top of this went the *audits*, comprising rubble or broken up concrete mixed with lime. The next layer, or *nucleus*, was a bedding of fine cement containing pounded potshards and lime. Finally the *dorsum*, the elliptical crown of the road curved for drainage, which was made up of large blocks of local stone. The bases of these blocks were sometimes cut to a point so as to bed more firmly into the *nucleus*. In towns, raised footways or pavements were constructed on either side of the road.

The Vía de la Plata cuts through the Iberian Peninsula from the Gulf of Cádiz to the Cantabrian coast. It was originally made up of a series of natural communication routes from Mérida on the Guadiana River to Astorga, the most northern of the Roman administrative centres, passing alongside rivers and through wide open valleys. The route went via Salamanca on the River Tormes and Zamora on the Duero, places which acted as the principal crossroads for traders travelling from east to west into what is now Portugal. Later, the Vía de la Plata extended north as far as Santiago de Compostela, serving also as a route for pilgrims who came from the south.

During the first century BC, the Romans, who built the paved road for the ever-increasing traffic in carts and chariots, began to extend the Vía de la Plata southwards to Itálica, near the modern city of Sevilla, to link up with their river transport.

Using the Guadalquivir, which at that time was navigable up to this point, everything was brought by boat to their oldest and largest settlement on the Iberian Peninsula.

Milarios, or milestones, some visible to this day, were set by the side of the route marking the Roman mile of 1480 metres or 1000 paces: a pace being two marching steps, left foot then right. The milestones, each weighing more than two tons, were circular pillars 1.50 metres high and 20cm in diameter on rectangular bases set 60cm into the ground. There is also evidence of the stopping places along the route every 25 to 30 kilometres, the distance normally travelled during a day's march and where remains of ancient settlements have been found, usually at the site of a natural spa or in a place that could easily be defended.

An outstanding example on the Vía de la Plata of these strategically-placed settlements is Acinipo, about 20 kilometres to the north-west of Ronda. From the highest point, at just under 1000 metres, there are extensive views over the surrounding land towards the Sierra de Grazalema to the west and the Serranía de Ronda to the east. Sentries posted along the natural high escarpment with its long, rocky drop would have been able to give ample warning of an approach made from any side.

Inhabited since Neolithic times, the site came under Roman rule in the 2nd century BC when it was considerably extended and also fortified by a perimeter wall, parts of which still exist. An amphitheatre was built at the highest point of the settlement with tiered seating for 2000 citizens. The lower levels, carved out of the natural bedrock, have endured the passing of time, abandonment and neglect. A large part of the main back wall also exists and, although spoiled by some unsightly 1980s concrete repair work, is a dramatic sight when looked at from wherever you are standing within the boundaries of Acinipo.

Extensive excavation work is still to be carried out, but what has been uncovered reveals the classic layout of a Roman settlement. The thermal baths, with their separate chambers for hot, cold or tepid bathing, are at the lowest point for easier access to water and for drainage. The two principal urban roads have also been discovered: the *Cardus*, running north-south, and the *Decumano* which went east-west. And from the few houses already excavated it can be seen that they were built in typical Roman style, with an atrium and several rooms surrounding a central patio.

For centuries the Vía de la Plata was the principle communication channel for political and economic life in western Iberia. In the mid-16th century, Felipe II established his Royal Court in Madrid which then became the capital of the Kingdom of Spain and thereafter the political and geographical centre of the country. Since that time all roads have tended to radiate from or encircle the capital. The north-south 'Silver Way' was all but abandoned.

As sections of the Vía de la Plata in Andalucía are gradually being reclaimed and restored, it is once again coming to life, this time as a rural route through stunning and varied landscapes. Many towns along the way are promoting it by emphasising the ancient artistic and ethnographic legacy left in this region by the myriad societies who have settled here. The route attracts not only lovers of nature but also those interested in the rich pattern of cultural and social history found along the way.

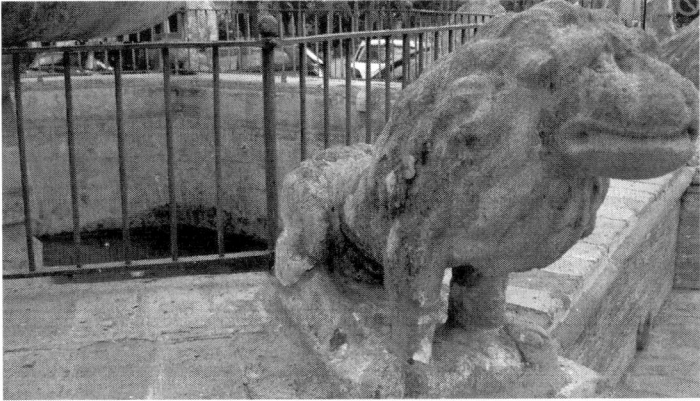

Lion fountain, Carmona

The Roman Way

The Vía Augusta was the principal paved road through Roman Hispania, the Iberian Peninsula. Named after Emperor Augustus, under whose mandate considerable improvements were made in the 8th to 2nd centuries BC, it went from Cádiz to the eastern Pyrenees, a distance of more than 1500 kilometres. Parts have endured for two millennia and are still visible. Some were still in use on stretches of the eastern coastal highway running beside the Mediterranean until the road was eventually asphalted in the early 20th century.

The Vía Baética, or Baetic Way, forms part of the Vía Augusta. It goes across the present day provinces of Cádiz, Sevilla and Córdoba and is one of the many cultural routes to pass through vestiges of the ancient Roman Empire in Andalucía.

Baética was roughly the area of contemporary Andalucía. When Hispania (known at the time as the *tierra de los conejos*, or land of rabbits) was divided up around the year 27 BC, it was the smallest but perhaps the most influential of the provinces of Imperial Rome. There were four regional jurisdictions: Hispalis (Sevilla); Gades (Cádiz); Cordvba (Córdoba); and Astigi (Écija); its capital the city of Córdoba. The area took its name from the river Betis, which the Moors subsequently called the Guadalquivir, meaning 'big river' in Arabic. It remained under Roman rule until the beginning of the 5th century and was later invaded by the Vandals and the Visigoths. When the Moors arrived early in the 8th century it became known as Al-Andalus.

In Roman times Baética was a rich agricultural region, known particularly for its wines, olive oil and cereals; also for *garum*, a fermented fish sauce much appreciated in the Roman diet. Amphorae from the area, in which these products were transported for export, have been discovered throughout most of what was the western Roman Empire.

The Guadalquivir River was navigable in the Roman era from Gadir – modern day Cádiz – up to Itálica, north-west of Sevilla. The city of Itálica, founded by Scipio in 206 BC, was named after its first inhabitants, wounded Italian soldiers who had fought in the battle of Ilipa against the Lusitanians. Later, under Hadrian, who succeeded Trajan as emperor, it became the largest Roman settlement in the Iberian Peninsula with the construction of the *nova urbs* on higher ground away from the river. But this 'new town' existed for only just over a hundred years before it was converted to agricultural land in the mid-3rd century AD. Many ruins of buildings were ploughed up and lost beneath the earth for centuries, with only a trace of the massive walls apparent among the fields. Extensive archaeological excavations began in the 18th century and still continue. Today visitors can truly get an idea of the wide paved roads, magnificent buildings, broad avenues, colonnaded pavements and splendid mosaics, along with one of the largest amphitheatres in the Roman Empire, which could seat up to 25,000 people.

The old part of Itálica by the river was inhabited by the Moors during their eight hundred-year rule and, when built over by the Christians in the 17th century, it became the town of Santiponce. From here the Baetic Way goes almost due east to Carmona. The origins of this delightful small city, arising arrestingly from the vast plain, date back to prehistoric times. Evidence has been found of human habitation from that era near the Corbonés River, one of the major tributaries of the Guadalquivir, but by the Bronze Age they had moved to higher ground, from where the settlement could be better defended. Taken from the Carthaginians by the Romans in 206 BC, Carmo, as they called it, became one of the most important urban centres in Baética and was granted the privilege of having its own coins of the same name.

Carmona was a walled city in Roman times, with four entrance gates. Two of these remain, though much renovated and changed over the centuries. The Puerta de Sevilla lies to the west and the Puerta de Córdoba to the east, the latter originally having three arches, a unique feature in Roman Hispania. Part of the bridge constructed to take the Vía Augusta over the Corbonés River exists outside the centre to the north-east and remains have been excavated under the present city of the forum and thermal baths. But it is the necropolis which is the jewel in Carmona's archaeological crown.

This extraordinary burial ground, constructed to the west of the city centre beside the Vía Augusta, was the largest Roman necropolis on the Iberian Peninsula. Discovered towards the end of the 19th century, it was the first archaeological site of its kind in Spain to be opened to the public. It covers a vast area and numerous chambers have been excavated, with evidence suggesting that cremation was customary. Of particular interest are two large tombs. The Tumba del Elefante, where a massive stone elephant was discovered in an extensive patio. The other, the Tumba de Servilia, has wall paintings of animals and vegetables that are some of the best preserved in Europe.

Travelling due east from Carmona, the Roman Baetic Way leads to the town of La Luisiana. Although officially founded in the 18th century by Carlos III and supposedly named after Luisa and Ana, two of his children, the area along the Carrión River had been settled for centuries. Many archaeological sites have been excavated, the Roman baths being the most important.

These baths were renovated soon after their discovery in the 18th century and used almost continuously well into the 20th century. There is also evidence nearby of several large Roman villas. Another find in La Luisiana was a *miliario*, which is now in the Archaeological Museum of Sevilla. Dating from the time of Emperor Constantine the Great, it was one of the 'milestones' placed along the Vía Augusta to mark every thousand paces.

East again to Astigi, now known as Écija, the capital of one of the four jurisdictions into which Roman Baética was divided. Astigi was an important centre for the production and export of olive oil, thanks to relatively easy transport via the Genil River to the Guadalquivir, then downstream to the port at Itálica. Records estimate that more than 20 million amphorae containing oil from this area went from Écija to Rome during the 1st to 3rd centuries AD.

Some of the most artistic and well preserved Roman mosaics discovered in Andalucía are exhibited in Écija's history museum, housed in the town's 18th-century Benamejí Palace. Of special interest, for the exquisite detail and use of colour, is the *Sacrifice of Dirce* and also the *Cortejo de Baco*, or *Courtship of Bacchus*, which shows various processes of turning grapes into wine. On display also are fragments of several granite columns, with carved marble Corinthian-style capitals. These came from the large forum found under the Plaza de España.

To the south of Écija lies the town of Osuna, known by the Romans as Urso, the Latin word for bear. Another Roman city to issue its own coins, those from Urso had a soldier in a helmet portrayed on the obverse and a bear tearing up a root from the ground on the reverse side. In today's town, parts of the Roman theatre and the water deposits still exist, but these are in privately-owned properties. In the public domain is an underground necropolis, used by the Romans but possibly dating to the Bronze Age. It was dramatically hewn out of the rock and has vaulted ceilings and paintings of birds on the walls.

From Osuna, part of the Roman Baetic Way goes north-west to Marchena and back to Carmona. In the 1st century BC Marchena became a Roman colony known as Colonia Marcia. Although the population was scarce, it was an important centre due to the agriculture carried out on the extensive undulating land lying between two tributaries of the Corbonés River. Some Roman mosaics, bronze rings and other relics have been uncovered, but few architectural remains have been found as the buildings were destroyed when the colony was conquered by the Moors.

Ancient dry-stone walling

The Bronze Way

In the eastern part of Andalucía, about 15 kilometres to the north of the city of Almería, there are significant remains of an early Bronze Age settlement. The archaeological site, known as Los Millares, is one of the most remarkable in Europe. It extends over approximately two hectares of land and dates from the end of the fourth century BC.

The location of this settlement was ideal. At the epicentre of ancient trading routes through southern Spain and on the edge of extensive lowlands, it was protected by high mountain ranges on almost every side. The rocky peaks of the Sierra Nevada rise up to the north-west, the softer Sierra de los Filabres to the north-east; Sierra Alhamilla is to the east with Sierra de Gador to the south-west. Abundant fresh water came from the melting snows in spring and rainwater run-off at other times of the year. The settlement was at the confluence of two major rivers. The Río Nacimiento (its name means the birth, or source), fed by its numerous mountain tributaries, flows down from the north; the Río Andarax from the west. Below this point the river is known as the Río Almería and flows through that city into the Gulf of Almería.

Los Millares was discovered in the late 19th century near the town of Santa Fé de Mondújar during the construction of the rail track. A settlement of roughly 1000 inhabitants, it appears to have been well guarded. Excavations have uncovered three surrounding concentric walls incorporating four bastions. A group of simple, round, stone dwellings stood within the walls, together with one large edifice which contained evidence of copper smelting.

Most of the inhabitants of Los Millares would, on the whole, have been farmers. However their society developed during what we now know was an important transition period in mankind's advancement after the Neolithic Age. Until then everything from drinking vessels to killing tools was hewn from stone and wood.

Now the craft of metal working was being discovered and enhanced. From subsisting as the hunters and gatherers of their forefathers, Bronze Age humans were evolving. At that time they began to settle in larger communities and to control the territories around them. Structures were constructed for lookouts and the defence of their settlements and for the collection of water; simple huts were erected for family living and for the initial practices of metallurgy.

In the first part of the second century BC the civilisation at Los Millares appears to have been replaced by the more advanced society of El Argar. The Argaric culture originated from the Mycenaean society of what is now Greece. Whereas their immediate predecessors had merely carried on the customs of those living there before them, the people of El Argar were more progressive. The new settlers created an important community at Antas, near Vera, in the most easterly part of present-day Andalucía and brought with them sophisticated methods of mining and metallurgy, burial rites and trade. Their distinct traditions and culture gradually extended through southern Iberia to Guadix, Baza and the region to the north and north-east of the Sierra de los Filabres, to Jaén and beyond.

Guadix lies at the crossroads of the Levantina and Bética regions, bordering the Guadalquivir river valley, between the coastal areas to the east and the mountainous territory to the north-west. It was an important enclave on a natural communication route through which, over many thousands of years, passed the commerce and culture of numerous civilisations. Legacies from the Roman and Moorish eras are more visible today, but evidence of human habitation dating to the Bronze Age has been found in the centre of the town.

The road to Baza from Guadix goes north-east through the beautiful mountain landscape of Sierra de Baza, now an environmentally protected area. Cutting through this nature reserve, roughly south to north, is the Río Gor. The cool, clear water springs out of the rocky quartz and marble terrain of the Sierra and tumbles down the deep, fertile canyon it has gouged out over the millennia. Here in this valley there are still signs of the ancient terraced meadows on both sides the river and of more than 200 dolmens, mainly around the town of Gorafe. Most date from the Neolithic era, but research has revealed that some of these burial sites were still in use during the early Bronze Age.

On a rocky spur, rising above a meandering loop of the Río Gor, is another of the many archaeological sites in the region: Las Angosturas. Its name, in Spanish geographical terms, means 'the narrows'. Although small, this settlement was so strategically placed that it was inhabited almost continuously from Neolithic times to the late Bronze Age around 600BC. From artefacts that have been discovered here, it seems it could have also been inhabited by the first Romans to arrive in the region during the 1st century BC.

A little further to the north of Las Angosturas, between the villages of Dehesas de Guadix and Villanueva de las Torres, there is another important site. Again in a well-planned position, La Terrera del Reloj lies at the junction of the Guadiana Menor and the Fardes rivers which flow east towards the Negratín reservoir. The mud and stone walls of the original terracing of the land have been found here along with many tombs, where the bodies of infants appear to have been placed in earthenware vessels before burial.

All the others discovered here were mainly in pits with evidence suggesting they were placed in a foetal position and surrounded by their 'grave goods' in the form of ceramic pots, metal ornaments and bronze weapons. And because of the type of materials unearthed and the social stratification inferred from analysis of the funerary goods and chattels, this settlement is very likely to have been part of the Argaric culture mentioned earlier.

Returning to Guadix and travelling due west, the main road leads to Purullena. The centre of this small town still retains the original Moorish layout with its narrow winding streets. On the outskirts there are numerous cave dwellings indicating much earlier inhabitants. Discoveries made at the nearby archaeological site of Cuesta del Negro have unearthed a fortified enclosure with a small necropolis, containing remains of some goods and chattels that date back to around 1800BC.

Going north now towards Jaén through the Parque Natural de Sierra de Huétor, there are other signs of prehistoric man. The rocky limestone terrain, with peaks rising to over 1800 metres, is sprinkled with numerous caves; the largest in the area, near the village of Piñar, being the Cueva de las Ventanas. Its name (cave with windows) derives from the three holes that give access to this vast underground space from the outside. Inhabited originally by Neanderthal man and used during the Bronze Age and later, its only residents now are occasional intrepid speleologists and thousands upon thousands of bats.

Jaén, the olive capital of Andalucía, rose to importance towards the end of the 2nd century BC during a short occupation by the Carthaginians. Hannibal's troops constructed a fortress on the top of the Cerro de Santa Catalina. There has been a fortress in one form or another on this high craggy hill ever since, dominating the modern city and the surrounding plain. Ceramic shards from the Bronze Age have been found on the higher areas of this rocky outcrop and there are some caves where rock paintings have been found, indicating they were lived in by prehistoric man. But it is on the lower slopes of Santa Catalina that significant ancient remains have been discovered.

Marroquíes Bajos, on the northern outskirts of Jaén, is an enormous archaeological site of more than 35 hectares. It has played an important role in understanding and recording the history of people living there thousands of years ago. The site takes its name from the Moors, the fourth and most recent of the ancient civilisations whose stratified remains have been discovered so far. The Moors built over the Roman city that had fallen into ruins and this, in turn, had been built upon Iberian and Chalcolithic settlements. The latter, also known as the Copper Age, was the transition period between Neolithic and Bronze eras when copper smelting and metallurgy was in its infancy.

Each civilisation tends to build over the previous one. There are already signs that future generations may find more precise ways of assessing the deeper, older remains without damaging the fragile structure of what lies above. When they do, a wealth of information about a society living more than four thousand years ago will be uncovered.

CULTURAL ROUTES

Path by stream in Granada

Moorish castle, Olvera

Introduction

Al-Andalus covered roughly the region now known as Andalucía. At the beginning of the 8th century the Umayyads arrived from Damascus and established themselves in Córdoba. From then until the end of the 15th century, when the kingdom of Granada was finally conquered by the Christians, it was a place where many different cultures and religions co-existed in relative harmony.

Cities such as Sevilla, Córdoba, Granada and Cádiz were recognised throughout Europe and North Africa at that time as centres of great learning. Renowned also for magnificent art and architecture, they were the home of great scientists and philosophers and were visited by travellers from far and wide.

After the Moors finally left southern Spain, their history and culture was soon forgotten by Spain and by Europe. The same fate faced the traditions and culture of the Jewish people who were expelled more or less at the same time. They were all relegated to legends in the annals of history, especially those eight centuries of Andalucía's past which were not considered to be of sufficient importance to be studied, or even remembered.

The cultural legacy from that time is now being brought to life by organisations such as the Fundación Legado Andalusí (Andalusian Legacy Foundation) and the Fundación Tres Culturas (Three Cultures Foundation). But the heritage of Al-Andalus does not only encompass Arab, Christian and Jewish cultures. As each civilisation tends to influence the one succeeding it in a subtle way, they in turn had been influenced by earlier settlers. The impact of the Moors, however, was stronger and is more apparent today than even that of the Romans.

As distances between the principal urban centres established by the Moors were so vast, numerous towns and villages sprung up along well-trodden routes connecting one to the other. These acted as staging posts, being settled by generations of caliphs and emirs, their families and entourages who built the *alcazabas* or citadels, *fortalezas* or fortresses, and the *castillos* that can still be seen today. Some have fallen into ruin; others have been restored to a greater or lesser degree, but all bear testimony to a fascinating period in the history of Andalucía.

The Fundación Legado Andalusí, a non-denominational cultural initiative, was set up in 1995 by the Junta de Andalucía. Its aims are to recover and disseminate the legacy of the Moorish, Christian and Jewish cultures which, for nearly eight centuries, illuminated not only Andalucía and the Iberian Peninsula, but also parts of the rest of Europe. This rich heritage encompasses the art and architecture still visible throughout the region and also embraces the sciences, including that of philosophy and logic, which were cultivated in a climate of religious and intellectual tolerance. The Foundation, which has the backing of UNESCO and the Council for Europe, among other public and private institutions, also focuses on promoting understanding and collaboration between the present-day Arab and western worlds.

Working on various fronts, in particular the organisation of educational programmes for children, the Foundation considers it important that the people of Andalucía and Spaniards in general are made more aware of those 800 years in their history. Its aim is that present and future generations embrace the period with pride. The majority of the population in southern Spain is, after all, directly descended from the people of Al-Andalus.

Documentation and publications on the history and culture of Andalucía include many comprehensive guides to its towns and cities, and the promotion of tourism plays an important role. To this end, one of the accomplishments of the Foundation has been the laying out and development of Las Rutas de Al-Andalus. These routes follow the paths taken by succeeding dynasties of Moors, from one end of Al-Andalus to the other. All lead to the magnificent mecca that is Granada, but first we come to Córdoba.

Puerta de Córdoba, Carmona

The road to Córdoba

The Ruta del Califato – Route of the Caliphs – connects Córdoba with Granada; the capital of the caliphs with the nucleus for the Nasrid dynasty. This was the one of the busiest pathways in the Iberian Peninsula during the Middle Ages. The two major cities at either end are beautiful and fascinating places to visit, but many ancient traces can be discovered along the way in isolated towns and villages set in spectacular landscapes.

From Córdoba, the first section of the Ruta del Califato is through the wide, fertile valley of the Guadalquivir River, either via Aguilar de la Frontera, Cabra and Priego de Córdoba, or the slightly more northern way to Castro del Río, Baena and Alcaudete. Both lead to Alcalá la Real. From here, since the terrain was so mountainous, the only way to Granada was via Moclín and Pinos Puente.

Alcalá la Real, a country town nestling at the foot of a hill, is dominated by a Moorish fort. Although later reconstructed by the Christians, one of the original entrance gates still exists: the Puerta de la Imagen.

Travelling south from Córdoba, just a few kilometres before reaching Águila de la Frontera, lies the town of Montilla. It was here that the Moors, despite their Prophet's prohibition, carried on the practice started by the Romans of cultivating the surrounding countryside for the growing of grapes. This tradition has continued virtually uninterruptedly for nearly two thousand years. In the first part of the 20th century most of the vintage went to Jerez de la Frontera to be marketed as sherry, but since the mid-1950s Montilla has had its own *denominación de origin*.

South again to Lucena, a centre of learning under the Moors. The town was taken by the Christians in 1240 and they subsequently built the Castillo del Moral over the ruins of an earlier castle. It was here in its tower, the Torre del Moral, that Boabadil, the last sultan of Granada, was imprisoned in 1483 for a short time. Turning north to Cabra, then east to Carcabuey, the route goes to Priego de Córdoba, which is unexpectedly full of splendid Baroque churches, though little remains of the city known as Medina Bahiga that flourished in Moorish times.

The first stop on the northern part of the Ruta del Califato, just 40 kilometres from Córdoba, is the white-walled village of Espejo. Here a Moorish castle looms over the cluster of dwellings, its austere lines appropriately mirroring the straight rows of olive trees and vineyards of the surrounding area. A mere nine kilometres away at Castro del Río is another castle, built by the Moors on the foundations of a Roman fort. Passing through Baena, a renowned olive oil production centre, the route wends its way into an area known as the Sierra Subbética de Córdoba. It goes to Doña Mencía and to Zuheros, with its romantic castle built into the rock, and Luque, where there is a 9th-century castle perched perilously on a rocky outcrop. Within the Parque Natural de las Sierras Subbéticas, where mountain peaks rise over 1300 metres and villages cling precariously to cliff sides, every curve in the road brings a different, awe-inspiring vista.

The sheer determination of the Moors, who carved out this route through the rugged landscape to reach Granada, has to be admired as it pushes on to Alcaudete. The town's 10th-century castle, boasting a massive keep, is the last stop before Alcalá la Real where there is a 13th-century fort. From here, the final part of the route goes through the mountainous terrain towards the splendid city of Granada.

Alcazaba, Antequera

From Tarifa to Granada

Andalucía and the countries of northwest Africa have much in common, not only historically and topographically, but also culturally. This is particularly apparent in the Magreb, a region now roughly comprising Morocco, Algeria and Tunisia, where much of the ancient architecture, art and artefacts are similar to what can still be seen in southern Spain.

The Ruta de Almorávides y Almohades – Route of the Almoravids and Almohads – begins in Tarifa and follows the tracks of those people of the Magreb who took their culture to the Iberian Peninsula. It was an era when trading caravans connected north and sub-Saharan Africa with the Mediterranean. Using the shortest crossing over the Strait of Gibraltar from the African continent, they landed in Tarifa. From here the route splits into two ways to Ronda. One takes the coastal route to Algeciras and San Roque, then heads north-east to the town of Jimena de la Frontera, Casares, Gaucín and villages up the Genal river valley. The other, longer route goes north from Tarifa to Alcalá de los Gazules and Medina Sidiona, then veers west to take in Cádiz and Jerez de la Frontera. It then turns almost due east to Arcos de la Frontera and Grazalema, and so through the high sierra to Ronda.

The town of Ronda straddles El Tajo, the impressive 130-metre gorge of the Guadalevín River. Before the arrival of the Moors it had been settled by the Romans and earlier by the Greeks and Phoenicians. Yet another example of a place where several cultures have met and merged. In the old town there is a spot from where you look through a Roman arch to a Moorish one and to a Christian church beyond. Much is left of the perimeter walls constructed by the Moors in the 13th century, in particular the Puerta de Almocábar to the south, the main entrance to the town at that time. Its name derived from Al-Maqabir, meaning cemetery, as it was the nearest exit to the outlying necropolis.

And so onwards to Granada… The Route of the Almoravids and Almohads goes north-east to Teba where, on Roman foundations, the Moors built an imposing castle. It is now mostly in ruins but has a well preserved dungeon. The route passes through the town of Campillos which officially came into being in 1492 by royal charter from the Catholic Kings. There is no evidence that the Moors settled here, though Roman remains have been discovered indicating significant pottery-making activities up to the 1st century AD. Then following the River Guadalhorce upstream, the route arrives at Antequera.

The Alcazaba dominates the town and is one of the best preserved medieval citadels in Spain. Part of its military defensive systems remains intact and stretches of the old walls surrounding what was the medina also still survive. But it is the huge Torre del Homenaje on the eastern corner which is of significant interest. Remodelled during the Nasrid dynasty, its configuration is almost that of a cube, being 17.26m by 17.44m and 17.08 metres high. The only other fortified tower of such size constructed by the Moors in Al-Andalus was the Torre de la Calahorra in Gibraltar. The bell tower and spire on top of the Torre del Homenaje were later additions, being built in 1582 by the Christians.

The Ruta de Almorávides y Almohades turns south from Antequera and goes through the fertile valley of the Vélez river. It arrives at Vélez-Málaga, which Moors named Ballix-Malaca, or the Fortress of Málaga, before going north once more.

The last stretch of this ancient route to Granada must have been the hardest, geographically. It goes through the ruggedly beautiful Axarquía region to Alcaucín from where, across a valley, you catch a glimpse of the deserted village of Zalía. Local legend has it that a Málaga priest, having tried unsuccessfully to convert the Moors to Christianity, sent a plague of vipers to attack the inhabitants. Beyond lie Zafarraya, at well over 1000 metres, and a stunning U-shaped cleavage in the Sierra de Alhama called the Puerto de Zafarraya. And so to the Gabias – Gabia La Grande and Gabia La Chica – before the journey's end in the city of Granada.

Puerta de la Justicia, Alhambra, Granada

In the Nasrid kingdom of Granada

The Ruta de los Nazaríes – Route of the Nasrids – goes from the town of Las Navas de Tolosa to Granada through many of the places that made up the defensive system of both Moors and Christians between the 13th and 15th centuries. The route passes by the ruins of watchtowers and castles, towers and turrets, many of them in the spectacular settings of the Sierra Morena and the Natural Park of Cazorla.

Proceeding south from Las Navas de Tolosa through La Carolina, the route bears west to Baños de la Encina, a sizeable village dominated by one of the most impressive Moorish castles in Andalucía. On a low hill above the castle is the 10th-century *alcázar*, or fortress, built at the behest of Al-Hakam II of Córdoba: an awe-inspiring sight, with its fourteen square towers and enormous keep. Looking east from here are magnificent views to the Sierra de Cazorla.

South again to Bailén where the Route of the Nasrids splits into two ways of reaching Jaén. One road goes east to Linares and then on to Baeza and Úbeda, both renowned for their Renaissance palaces and mansions, but where precious little has survived of Moorish art and architecture. Crossing the wide Guadalquivir river valley the route takes you to Jódar and then Jimena and Mancha la Real.

The other road from Bailén goes west to Andújar, crossing its fifteen-arched bridge originally built by the Romans and subsequently greatly restored by the Moors. South to Arjona and then south-west to Porcuna. Named Ipolka by the Iberians who first settled there, it has the remains of a large fortified tower. The last Moorish leader, Muhammed XII, known to the Spanish as Boabdil was apparently briefly imprisoned here in the 1480s during the battle for Lucena.

In 1975, just outside the present urban area in Cerrillo Blanco, more than 1500 fragments of mutilated sculptures from the 5th century BC were discovered. They are now on display in the museum at Jaén. From Porcuna the route goes to Torredonjimeno and then Martos, before turning east again through Torredelcampo and on to Jaén.

The name Jaén derives from the Arabic *geen*, meaning a stopping place on a caravan route. Settled by the Moors in the 8th century, the city boasts the largest *hamman*, or steam baths, to survive in Spain. Hot springs in the area, discovered first by the Romans, were subsequently used by the Moors to build a series of public baths and the carefully preserved *hamman* that can be seen today originally formed part of an 11th-century palace.

The baths fell into disuse after the *Reconquista* and in the 16th century the Palacio de Villadompardo was constructed over them. After being re-discovered in the early 20th century, they were restored in the 1980s. Now the visitor can walk through the various rooms, used formerly for cold, tepid and hot bathing, and gaze at the ancient brickwork ceilings, star-shaped windows and elegant horseshoe arches.

Leaving Jaén, the Ruta de los Nazaries heads south towards Granada through mountainous terrain, where some of the peaks reach more than 1500 metres. The route goes to Cambil, Huelma and Guadahortuna, before turning south-west to reach Piñar where there is an unusual castle that has round as well as square towers. Built by the Romans, the castle was subsequently added to, rather than reconstructed, by the Moors, becoming a strategic defensive point for the Nasrids who were in the control of commercial trade between Jaén and Almería.

Piñar was a principal gathering place of pre-historic man and remains found in the Cueva de la Carigüela date back to 20,000 BC. On to Iznalloz, whose name means *monte de los almendros*, the hill of almonds, and to Deifontes. Both places formed part of the defensive line for the Nasrid Empire. Finally, the route turns south to take in Albolote and Macarena before the last short stretch into the city of Granada.

Granada, the jewel in the architectural crown of the Moorish dynasty ... It was chosen by most of their rulers as the centre of power in Al-Andalus, a place where they constructed magnificent palaces and opulent mansions. They recovered and extended the irrigation systems laid out by the Romans, which had fallen into disuse after their departure. Water was brought into the very heart of buildings through a complex network of wells and channels, fountains and pools and not only for domestic use. It was also used extensively as an ornamental feature in public squares and private gardens and patios, and to supply the numerous public baths which formed an integral part of their culture.

The *pièce de resistance* of Granada is the Alhambra, considered the epitome of Nasrid architecture. Originally a complete government city, it had mosques and mansions, schools and army barracks, as well as large areas of formal gardens such as the incomparable Generalife. The Alcazaba and the Palacios Nazaríes (Nasrid palaces), where Arabic inscriptions feature prominently and decorative ceramics abound, remain nearly seven centuries later as testimony to their constructive artistry.

It was from this magnificent centre of culture, of science and learning, of glorious art and architecture, that Boabdil was expelled when the armies of Fernando and Isabel, the *Reyes Católicos* or Catholic Kings, finally took the city of Granada. In 1492 they raised the Christian cross on the Alcazaba, alongside their royal standards of Castilla and Aragón.

When forced out from their last stronghold in Spain, the Nasrids travelled with their leader Boabdil to the Alpujarras. They were allowed to settle temporarily in an area on the south-facing slopes of the Sierra Nevada, but not for long ...

Alhambra Towers

From Granada into exile

Boabdil, who had been born in the Alhambra Palace at Granada in the mid-15th century, became king in 1482 when he was in his early twenties. Called *el rey chico* (the little king), this had nothing to do with his stature but the ever-diminishing size of his dynasty. He was also known as *el zogoybi* (the unfortunate one) due to his brief career, doomed to end in exile, as the last monarch of the Nasrids.

A year after having deposed his father, he tried to invade Castilla only to be taken prisoner in the castle at Lucena. In exchange for his liberty, three years later Boabdil settled for governing Granada as a vassal state under the Catholic kings. His throne was returned to him, but it was to be a short-lived rule. The city of Granada, after eight centuries under the Moors, finally capitulated at the beginning of January 1492, bringing the Christian *Reconquista* to completion. Boabdil was subsequently granted a fiefdom in the Alpujarras.

He left Granada with his family and a few hundred faithful followers and retainers. Before passing through the mountain pass to La Zubia, he paused, looked back and sighed for what he had lost. The Puerto del Suspiro del Moro is the last place from which he could still see his birthplace, his palace and his kingdom.

The route Boabdil travelled went south to Lanjarón, gateway to Las Alpujarras, which lies at the south-western end of the Sierra Nevada. The town was originally settled by the Romans who discovered seven natural springs in the area. It continues to be well known as a spa, also for its mineral water and the first place in Spain to bottle it.

Turning east, the route to the land ceded to Boabdil at Láujar de Andarax winds its way along the northern side of the wide Guadalfeo River basin. Long, narrow, tree-lined valleys extend up into the sierras to Capileira and Bubión, Pitres and Pórtugos; white-washed villages that appear to have remained in a time warp for centuries, and to Trévelez, the highest urban conurbation in Spain and renowned for its hams.

The Alpujarras stretch west to east through the provinces of Granada and Almería. Protected by the high sierras to the north and the lower sierras of Gador, La Contraviesa and Lújar to the south, the region avoids the worst of the winter weather.

The relentless descent of water from the Sierra Nevada has, over the centuries, brought down abundant silt that has been deposited over the hills and grassy plains. Snow from the mountains melts during late spring and early summer keeping the villages supplied with fresh water throughout the year.

The Moors had an innate knowledge of agriculture and also brought with them their engineering skills to lay out complex networks of *acequias*, or irrigation channels. They repaired and maintained the mountainside terracing, which had fallen into disuse after the Romans left, and turned the Alpujarras into a garden paradise.

Boabdil lived for less than a year in Láujar de Andarax. Not content with a tranquil life he travelled to Fez in Morocco where he fought many other battles and died in 1527. The majority of his followers stayed behind until they, in turn, were expelled around 1570. Two Moorish families in each village were, however, forced to remain so they could instruct the incoming Christian peasants in matters of agriculture and water management.

CULTURAL HERITAGE

Convento de San Francisco, Granada

Alcazaba de la Alhambra, Granada

Introduction

Andalucía's cultural heritage is now more visible as Moorish and Renaissance palaces are being preserved, olive mills converted into museums and historic monuments unearthed. Some are being carefully restored; others lie anonymously in ancient towns and country areas awaiting recognition. Many more, having remained undiscovered for centuries, are revealed when modern roads cut through the land.

UNESCO, the United Nations Education, Science and Culture Organisation, defines our heritage as 'the legacy we have received from the past, how we are living in the present, and what we transmit to future generations'. The aim of this international organisation is to identify, protect and preserve unique forms of natural and cultural inheritance considered of special value to humanity.

There are UNESCO world heritage sites all over the world and, since the early eighties, the organisation has recognised nearly 40 cultural and natural assets in Spain. In Andalucía, among the first sites to be acknowledged were the Alhambra Palace, the Generalife and the Albaicín district, all in Granada, as well as the historic town centre of Córdoba. That was in 1984. Since then, the cathedral at Sevilla and the Coto Doñana National Park were granted recognition in 1987 and 1994 respectively and, in 2003, the towns of Úbeda and Baeza, with their myriad Renaissance palaces, were added to the prestigious list.

As one civilisation builds upon another, the intrinsic features of each mix and merge. What we think of now as typically Spanish characteristics: the whitewashed houses, beautiful arched doors and windows, tiled courtyards and fountains; these were all handed down from much older cultures.

Large urban centres such as Córdoba, Granada or Málaga have grown and thrived over the centuries under a variety of rulers and cultures. They have been formed from what they inherited and adapted in every aspect of life: art and architecture, language and music, fashion and food, customs and traditions. In Roman times the countryside surrounding the towns was laid out with olive groves, wheat fields and vineyards. The Moors channelled water from the mountains to irrigate their crops and vegetable gardens. Many of the original agricultural customs are still practised today and ancient terracing for grape vines and almond trees is still visible on many mountainsides, though much has been lost to development and the abandonment of small farms in the hinterland.

The topographical, or natural, aspect of Andalucía is much the same as it was in pre-historic times. Even though river courses have altered, estuaries have silted up and marshland has been reclaimed, the sierras and the plains are relatively unchanged. But much of the countryside has been ravaged. Whole forests were cleared for building ships and houses, or have been destroyed by fire. Mountainsides have been scarred by quarries in the constant quest for stone. Sustainable development, working with and safeguarding the natural resources we have today, in order to be able to pass them on to the next generations, is the greatest hope for the future if we are to conserve our natural heritage.

Casino Gaditano, Cádiz

Urban legacies

They came, they saw, they conquered. Not just the Romans, and before them the Phoenicians, but the Visigoths, Moors and Catholics. Centuries of traders, invaders and city planners, all eager to impose their own imprints on the cities they took over. They re-used much of the fabric of what they destroyed and in the process created what we now regard as typical Spanish architecture.

Many features come from different centuries and different cultures. The Giralda tower in Sevilla was originally a Moorish minaret. The Albaicín, the old Moorish quarter of Granada, grew out of the Roman city. The foundations of Málaga were built over the ancient *ashlars* of the first Phoenician settlements. In the centre of Cádiz a wealthy 19th-century merchant constructed his home with an inner patio imitating the *mudéjar*-style of architecture. The building now houses the Casino Gaditano, a private club.

The give and take of Andalucía's urban heritage is apparent in all its big cities. But nowhere is it more aesthetically appealing than in Córdoba.

Within the massive, mellow brick walls of the Grand Mosque, avenues of columns and intricate arches stretch almost as far as one can see. The small synagogue delights the eye with delicate decoration, and narrow streets with white-washed walls and flower-strewn courtyards have enraptured generations of artists and photographers. Beyond the historic centre, the buzzing new city, with its wide streets and elegant modern buildings, still echoes the old in colonnaded gateways, palm-shaded squares cooled by tiled fountains, and private courtyards paved in patterned marble. Styles have amalgamated over the centuries to create a harmonious whole.

One of the first things a new owner usually does to a house these days is up-date the décor. The Moors were no different. Abd ar-Rhaman, the last surviving Umayyad prince from distant Damascus, did it on a grand scale after he arrived in Córdoba in 756 when the city had already been occupied by his kinsmen for 40 years. Living among Visigothic Christians on the site of the Roman capital of Baética, they shared as a place of worship a fine cathedral dedicated to San Vicente. Delicately carved capitals topped old Roman columns taken from the temple over which it was built. The roof was supported by horseshoe arches which were then unknown in Arab architecture.

Abd ar-Rhaman was inspired. He rebuilt the old Roman bridge, constructed mills, whose ruins can still be seen on the northern bank of the then-navigable Guadalquivir river, and successfully organised agriculture, commerce and communications. Once the infrastructure of the city was under way, he turned his attention to making Córdoba a centre of learning, leisure and, most of all, spiritual fulfilment. The focal point was the mosque.

Based partly on the memories of his past heritage, of the mosques of Damascus and Jerusalem, Abd ar-Rhaman incorporated the pillars and other ideas from the Visigothic cathedral. His architects made their own brilliant interpretation of the horseshoe arch. The new mosque had eleven aisles open to the courtyard at the north-west, where eleven corresponding rows of orange trees drew the worshipper inside. Natural light shone onto the arches, gleaming like the rays of the sun in alternating red brick and white stone, fanning out above a variety of ancient columns of white marble, jasper and granite.

The mosque was extended later to accommodate the larger population, and succeeding Moorish rulers added more aisles, columns (now more than 850) and ever-more intricate arches. Today it is three times its original size; very different, but still stunning.

The position of the *mihrab*, which never faced Mecca but Abd ar-Rhaman's home city of Damascus, is now intriguingly asymmetric because of major enlargements in the 9th and 10th centuries which extended eastwards. Rebuilt after the last extension with the help of Byzantine craftsmen, its rich pattern of mosaics and the ribbed vaulting were to influence future metropolitan architecture throughout Spain and, some say, Gothic architecture throughout Europe.

For more than a century after the Reconquest, Christians worshipped in the mosque without modifying it. Eventually, a small chapel was built within the forest of pillars in 1371 and the interior of the mosque was walled off from the patio. But the greatest change of all was made in the 16th century with the building of a Renaissance cathedral right at its heart.

Carlos V, King of Spain and Holy Roman Emperor, sanctioned the work but realised his mistake when he saw it: "You have destroyed something that was unique in the world," he reprimanded those responsible for the building. Perhaps he was too harsh; the intrusion appears now to be an acceptable part of its history. And the mosque has never lost its feeling of universal spirituality going back beyond its early roots to Roman and Phoenician beginnings. Today, most visitors go to marvel at its architecture rather than to worship. But whatever their beliefs, they cannot fail to be moved by this unique testament to compromise.

El Torcal, Antequera

Natural environment

El Torcal, one of the most impressive karstic limestone regions in Europe, was the first natural area in Andalucía to be officially protected. Fifty years later, in 1978, it was recognised as a nature reserve. Extending over more than 1000 hectares, the wind-whipped mountain range, which shelters the town of Villanueva de la Concepción from the winter weather, contains surrealistic rocky sculptures and is home to abundant flora and fauna.

Over the centuries the rocky outcrops have been moulded by the wind and the rain into shapes engendering names such as El Tornillo, the screwdriver, or El Dedo, the finger.

It is an eerie and wild landscape, with boulders teetering atop each other or lying around like stone toys thrown down by raging baby giants. Rising from Spain's inland *meseta*, or tableland, to the highest peak of Camorra Alto at 1369 metres above sea level, it forms part of the Sierras Subbéticas, the mountain ranges running in an east-westerly direction from Jaén to Cádiz.

The calcareous or limestone landscape is characterised by cracks and canyons, channels and gulleys that have been formed by rainwater and underground water dissolving the calcium carbonate in the rock. This results in the roofs of subterranean caves collapsing on top of one another and underground streams continually seeking other downhill routes. Above ground, erosion from the wind and the rain has resulted over the centuries in a slowly changing assortment of the wonderful natural sculptures we see today.

Inhabited since prehistoric times, the resources of the area were used more or less in a sustainable manner up to the 19th century. But with the arrival of the so-called industrial 'revolution' the area became exploited by mankind to an almost disastrous level. Trees were felled for their timber and for charcoal burning, quarries were a hive of activity in the extraction of stone for building, and what natural pastures and grassland remained were used for intense grazing of animals. All of this combined to hinder the regeneration of natural vegetation. The result was that the aspect of higher parts of the Natural Park remains desolate to this day, as there are virtually no trees to soften the bleakness.

Despite this human interference, the area is rich in an immense variety of flora and fauna. El Torcal is credited with no less than 664 species of plants, more than 80 different birds, and numerous reptiles and small mammals. Many of the birds, such as eagles, peregrine falcons and vultures are resident all the year. But the craggy peaks are also used as a nesting place for feathered visitors and a stopping-off point for various migratory species en route from Africa to northern Europe. You can walk to the Mirador de las Ventanillas, past electric blue irises hiding under stunted yellow gorse. From this viewpoint, with the town of Villanueva de la Concepción visible far below you, the Spanish and the African coastlines of the Mediterranean can be seen on a very clear day in the far distance.

In the south-western corner of Andalucía is another important area of natural heritage: the Coto Doñana National Park. Stretching through the provinces of Huelva and Sevilla and encompassing part of the Guadalquivir river basin, it is one of the most important wetland areas in Europe. UNESCO added the park to its list of World Heritage sites in 1994, acknowledging it to have 'exceptional universal value'.

Doñana covers nearly 54,000 hectares of land and is one of the most significant ecological regions in Europe. Many species of animal, such as lynx, deer and wild boar, share this great wilderness all the year round. They are joined by more than 200,000 migratory birds, which either arrive in late autumn to spend the winter away from cold northern climates, or in the spring to seek their traditional breeding grounds.

Named the Wada-I-Kebir (the big river) by the Moors, the Guadalquivir has an extensive delta which is part of Doñana. For centuries it has been increasingly isolated from the sea by a gigantic sandbar. This begins at the mouth of the Río Tinto, near Palos de la Frontera, and extends to the western bank of the big river just across from the town of Sanlúcar de Barrameda. Thrashed by stormy weather off the sea, the high sand dunes along the coast now form a natural barrier for the marshes. The lower, inland dunes are constantly on the move.

The winds catch their crests and blow the fine-grained sand in an inexorable march towards the pine forests, engulfing their trunks, depriving their roots of moisture and eventually overwhelming them.

The marshes stretch out to an infinite horizon in an extraordinary merging of land and water. The area is a haven of tranquillity for resident and migratory wildlife and immensely fertile. It is fed by minerals brought down from the far-away mountains of the Sierra Cazorla, where the Guadalquivir has its source, and from its innumerable tributaries that fan out over great distances west and east.

Together with the adjoining pine forests, this wild, uninhabited region was owned for nearly five hundred years by successive dukes of Medina Sidonia and became the favoured hunting grounds of kings and princes. The seventh duke constructed an isolated palace there at the end of the 16th century for his duchess, Doña Ana de Silva y Mendoza, and the area has been known as 'Doñana' ever since.

Because of its unique environmental importance, much scientific interest had been shown in the region since before the beginning of the 20th century. It was not until 1969 though that Doñana was given the status of National Park and became an officially protected environment.

Another wetland area, the Laguna de Fuente de Piedra (Lagoon of the Stone Spring), lies to the north-west of Antequera, just off the road to Estepa and not far from the small town from which it takes its name. At 400 metres above sea level, it extends over 1550 hectares and is one of the largest natural lakes in Spain. From remains found nearby it is apparent that the area was inhabited by the Iberians and Phoenicians and possibly even earlier. When the Romans settled there in the 2nd century, they referred to the spring of water as the *fons divinus*, or divine spring, in recognition of the medicinal properties of the saline waters which bubbled up from below.

Around the mid-16th century, the authorities in Antequera decided to create a community near the spring, where people suffering from kidney problems could stay and 'take the waters'. This also contributed to an influx of commerce in the area, based not only on the health-giving benefits provided by the water, but also on the salt industry that had grown in importance. The lagoon then became known as the Laguna Salada or Salt Lake. Still to be seen are several structural formations from those days, such as the dykes made to channel the water outwards from the marsh to aid in the crystallisation of the salt.

Fierce droughts throughout the 18th century resulted in the lake drying out to such an extent that the stagnant waters contributed to the increase of epidemics. The resulting foul air caused much havoc throughout the region. Despite many attempts to rid the area of the health hazard, the lagoon remained virtually abandoned for a long time. It was not until the mid-1980s that the idea was mooted to try to find the original spring, clean up the surrounding area and recover the lagoon. In 1982 it was included in the list of wetlands of international importance under the Ramsar Convention and it was recognised in 1988 as a *Zona de Protección Especial para las Aves* – an area of special protection for birds.

The Laguna de Fuente de Piedra was declared a Nature Reserve in 1989 and, thanks to the success in the general protection of this natural area, the lagoon has become one of the largest breeding grounds for the flamingo in the Mediterranean.

UNESCO also monitors and protects innumerable natural regions under the MAB programme (Man and the Biosphere) that is becoming ever more important as the world's natural resources are used up. The biosphere, that part of Earth's immediate outer shell including the air, land, surface rocks and water, is where life occurs. It is, broadly, the global ecological system integrating all living beings and their relationships, and includes their interaction with the elements. Biosphere reserves are made up of core protected areas, surrounded by buffer zones where only limited human activity is allowed.

The Sierra de las Nieves, that dramatic limestone mountain range protecting the town of Marbella from the north winds, was designated in 1995 as a biosphere reserve. From Istán and Ojén in the south, to El Burgo and Casarabonela in the north, it covers nearly 94,000 hectares and rises to more than 1900 metres above sea-level.

Due to the extreme changes in altitude throughout the area, the Sierra de las Nieves presents a unique variety of Mediterranean ecosystems. At its heart are the delightful villages of Monda and Guaro, whose surrounding countryside is air-brushed in spring with delicate pink and white almond blossom, like confetti fallen from the sky. It is a place where ospreys and wildcats, river otters and roe deer can be seen by those who are patient and know where to look. And, at higher altitudes, there remain a few small forests of the Spanish fir *(abies pinsapo)* found only here, at Grazalema and in the Sierra Bermeja behind Estepona.

The aim in a biosphere reserve is to conserve and improve the natural and cultural heritage and to allow mankind to work together with nature. The principal research and monitoring of this reserve are administered by the universities of Málaga and Sevilla. To avoid fragmented decision-making, a consortium was also set up comprising representatives from the ten municipalities whose land is included in the reserve. Agricultural activities and forest production are being supported, rural tourism is promoted and age-old country traditions and customs are encouraged. Sustainable development is the keyword so present generations can benefit from and enjoy what they have, at the same time conserving it for future generations.

Palacio de Carlos V, Granada

Renaissance monuments

The expulsion of the Moors from Spain coincided with another momentous development in fifteenth century Europe: the Renaissance. Empires were being formed, trade was increasing and notable families were influencing art and architecture.

The old order was being questioned. Once *renaissance* (literally 'rebirth') took hold, the movement spread quickly to countries previously forming the western Roman Empire. This rebirth of classicism, which began early in that century in what is now Italy, took much of its inspiration from ancient Greece and Rome.

The Renaissance came much later to Andalucía. And here it was different as it demonstrated also the celebration of the rebirth of Christianity after eight centuries of Islamic rule. Moorish architecture had perhaps reached its peak in Andalucía. But, like all great flowerings of civilisation, its day had passed. Architects working for the new Christian rulers were able to rejoice in the freedom to use representations of the human form, which had not allowed by Muslim authorities.

One of the first commissions to be ordered in Granada by the conquering kings, after their *reconquista* in 1492, was their future tomb. The Capilla Real or Royal Chapel, one of the city's most impressive Christian buildings, is where Fernando el Católico was laid to rest in 1516 alongside his wife Isabel la Católica who died in 1504.

Ferdinand and Isabella had quickly laid the foundation for the future political unification of Spain under their grandson, Emperor Charles V. When he subsequently became King Carlos I of Spain he continued the process of 'Christianisation' of architecture started by his grandparents. Shortly after commissioning the magnificent Palacio de Carlos V, he left Granada for good and the palace, which was begun in 1526, was never finished. It was not until the 1960s that the coffered ceilings of the colonnade were added; until then the Ionic columns had reached up to an open sky. Granada never became the seat of Spanish monarchy as Carlos I had planned, but it was, however, turned into a palatial city with the help of the greatest architect of that time, Diego de Siloé.

Siloé, who was born in Burgos in 1495, had travelled to Italy in his early twenties to study Renaissance art and architecture in Naples. On returning to his native town, he created in 1519 one of his most important works, the *escalera dorada,* or golden staircase, which he built in the city's cathedral. The perfectly proportioned and elegantly curved structure, with its cherubim, heraldic shields and decorative ornamentation, occupies the whole of one wall.

He moved south to Granada in 1528 and worked there until the end of his life in 1563. Here, his main projects were the construction of the church in the Convento de San Jerónimo and of the city's cathedral; work on the latter being entrusted to him in 1529 and finished eight years later. One of its main features is the enormous central area covered with a huge cupola, a design he possibly conceived after seeing Filippo Brunelleschi's work in Florence, in particular the Italian architect's splendid cupola in the Santa Maria dei Fiori church in Florence. Another outstanding aspect of Granada's cathedral, built around 1534, is the Portada del Perdón, literally the 'entrance gate of forgiveness'. Created on the lines of a great triumphal arch, its flowing curves and intricate carvings are a classic example of the uniquely Spanish Plateresque style, described later.

The city of Granada is regarded as a model of imperial architecture. The churches in many surrounding provincial towns are proof of the building extravaganza undertaken by bishops and ecclesiastical councils following in the wake of the avalanche of conversions to Christianity – voluntarily or otherwise – of most of the population.

The parish churches in Iznalloz, to the north of Granada, and in Loja to the east, are just two Renaissance examples, both designed by Siloé. And in Antequera there is the Collegiate Church of Santa María la Mayor. Built around 1550, again to Siloé's plans, the façade is Plateresque, and inside it features three wide naves separated by Ionic columns with *mudéjar*-style chapels on either side.

This is a typical example of the changes that were taking place in architectural ideas during the 16th century. Still reflecting Roman ideals, they incorporated ideas of the time and predicted the richly ornate designs of what was to become Baroque.

Mudéjar was a new form of architecture for Christians living in 16th-century Andalucía, but one which incorporated the influences, elements and materials of Hispano-Muslim design. The term is derived from the Arabic meaning: 'what has been allowed to remain' or 'those who accept submission'. Architecturally it is a phenomenon native to the area and exclusively Hispanic. Its influence survived in Andalucía well into the 17th century.

Málaga cathedral is also the work of Diego de Siloé. Or rather, it was built according to plans he drew up. Construction, which began under his supervision in 1528, continued for more than 250 years. Siloé was brought in to modify the plans in 1541 and the work was subsequently continued by other Andalusian Renaissance architects including Diego Vergara and Andrés de Vandelvira.

The north tower, an emblematic landmark of the city, is 87 metres high, making the cathedral the second highest in Andalucía after the one in Sevilla. The south tower, however, was never erected as the money allocated to this and to many other projects in Málaga was diverted towards developing Spain's American colonies. It remains with only one tower to this day, its lopsided appearance resulting in the local nickname of La Manquita – the one-armed lady.

There is evidence of the revival of classical Greek and Roman design in Renaissance architecture. This is found in the orderly arrangements of colonnades or long rows of round columns, and in the pilasters, the flattened and slightly projecting columns built into or onto walls. Plans of buildings were based on square, symmetrical forms. Façades, especially those of the churches, were generally surmounted by a pediment and organised by a system of pilasters, arches and entablatures. The use of semicircular arches was apparent as was the placing, wherever possible, of niches to hold religious images.

Hemispherical domes were another salient feature of this time. Up to then domes had not been widely used, but now they appeared frequently in churches and palaces, military buildings and private mansions. Wider in span and higher than before, due to new construction skills, they were visible from the outside as an imposing feature.

Columns, used for structural or purely decorative purposes, were similar to those seen in ancient Rome. Delicately wrought pilasters were grafted on to flat Gothic façades creating designs that were much more ornate compared to the austere forms of Moorish architecture.

Characterised by fine ornamental details which were carved out with great precision, this decorative style became known as Plateresque, the term deriving from the intricate work carried out by the *plateros* or silversmiths. In addition, an elaborate *retablo* (literally a 'board behind') became a common feature of churches and cathedrals. These decorative panels, or ledges, were usually placed behind an altar, but occasionally also on exterior walls.

Málaga cathedral

Golden Age architecture

The 16th century was essentially the Siglo de Oro, the Golden Age, when arts, literature and culture in general flourished in Spain. It was the time of Miguel de Cervantes, author of *El Ingenioso Hidalgo Don Quijote de La Mancha*, known universally as *Don Quijote* and considered one of the finest works in European literature.

Luis de Góngora was a prominent figure in Golden Age poetry. He lived most of his life and wrote most of his important works in Córdoba. Lope de Vega, a prolific writer and literary contemporary of Cervantes, laid down the structures and genres of Spanish drama.

Pedro Calderón de la Barca was a playwright *par excellence*, whose death in 1681 is said to mark the end of the Siglo de Oro. And in art there were, of course, the old masters: El Greco and Velázquez.

Jaén's cathedral stands out as a remarkable example of the assertive power of Catholic Spain of that era and the cities of Úbeda and Baeza are the jewels in Andalucía's Renaissance crown with at least 50 glorious monuments still standing as witness to the Siglo de Oro. Having flourished during Spain's age of enormous riches, they were forgotten during centuries of persecution and poverty. History passed them by. Left as they were, it is only relatively recently they have achieved the recognition they deserve. In 2003, Úbeda and Baeza became a joint UNESCO World Heritage site.

During the Siglo de Oro, Spain was at the forefront of innovation. Almost everything that was introduced was copied and imitated with great fervour elsewhere in Europe. Learning the Spanish language was much in fashion. Colombus had discovered the New World and the fleets making forays westwards brought back with them untold riches to furnish and decorate Spanish churches, palaces and stately homes.

It was also a creative and productive time for the new style of Renaissance architecture. Diego Siloé, already mentioned, was a renowned architect in Málaga and Granada and much of Andrés de Vandelvira's work remains in all its golden glory in the northern Andalusian cities of Jaén, Úbeda and Baeza. But one name from that time stands out from the rest, not least because of the continuity of three generations of the same family, is Hernán Ruiz.

Hernán Ruiz Rodríguez – known as El Viejo or 'the old one' to distinguish him from his son and grandson of the same name – came to Córdoba from Burgos at the beginning of the 16th century. With the Renaissance movement beginning to spread throughout Andalucía this was a time of great architectural change. The plain, straight lines, with little decoration, favoured by the Moors who had ruled in the region for nearly eight centuries, was giving way to curves and rich ornamentation.

One of the principal examples marking this artistic transition was attributed to El Viejo. The old Hospital Mayor de San Sebastián in Córdoba (now housing the Palacio de Congresos) is considered a work of 'humanist Gothic'. Built around 1514, for more than 200 years it was the most important health centre in the province. Apart from the entrance portico, Ruiz also designed the heart of the building with cloisters built in the *mudéjar* style and a flamboyantly Gothic chapel, rich in Plateresque decoration.

When Hernán El Viejo died in Córdoba in 1547 he left behind him a family tradition of architects whose work would be admired and visited for centuries. His son, Hernán Ruiz Jiménez, is the most well known. Called, logically, Hernán Ruiz II, he was known universally as El Mozo or 'the young lad'. He was born in 1514 and became one of the most prominent architects in Renaissance Andalucía. Qualifying in Córdoba in 1530 as an *alarife*, or master architect, in his early years his work was mainly centred in that city and province. He designed civil and religious constructions, public and private buildings, *ingenios* or sugar mills, and numerous works of urban infrastructure such as communication and hydraulic systems. He also wrote countless articles regarding building matters and drew up plans most prodigiously.

Córdoba had been conquered by the Catholic Kings more than two centuries previously and ecclesiastical notables had long wished to pursue their dream of 'Christianising' the magnificent Grand Mosque built by the Moors. Although a *mudéjar*-style Capilla Real, or Royal Chapel, had already been installed by Alfonso X in the late 13th century, it was thought that by adding a *coro* (choir stalls) and a *capilla mayor* (main chapel) the building could be finally made into an important place of worship for Christians. Eventually they found a monarch who was willing to sanction the work: Carlos V.

In his so-called Christian zeal, this king had already built over or partially destroyed other Moorish constructions such as the Alcázar in Sevilla or Granada's Alhambra Palace. Hernán Ruiz El Viejo had begun work on the Coro and Capilla Mayor in 1523, but it was his son, El Mozo, who carried it to fruition. Coincidentally it was the third architect in this family, Hernán Ruiz Díaz, who was to be responsible at the end of the 16th century for renovating the Patio de los Naranjos and the bell tower at the Mosque in Córdoba.

Hernán Ruiz, El Mozo, also designed buildings throughout the provinces of Cádiz and Sevilla. He produced the blueprints for a bridge across the river Guadalete at Arcos de la Frontera and for the Convent of Santo Domingo in Sanlúcar de Barrameda, where the first duke and duchess of Medina Sidonia were laid to rest in the 17th century.

In Jerez de la Frontera he was responsible for drawing up plans for the churches of San Juan and San Miguel, the latter with its Isabelline / Gothic-style portico, and for the collegiate church of El Salvador. And in Villamartín, a town on the banks of the Guadalete, he designed the parish church of Nuestra Señora de las Virtudes. Its tall, slender bell-tower, similar in design to La Giralda in Sevilla, stands proud but seemingly apart from the main building.

But much of the work for which El Mozo is renowned lies in Sevilla, where he lived from 1558 until his death eleven years later. Employed towards the end of December 1557 as *Maestro Mayor*, or Grand Master, of the city's cathedral, it took him less than two weeks to produce the plans for the new Sala Capitular (Chapter House) and the elevated extension of La Giralda tower. From then on there was no stopping him.

In 1560 he drew up plans for the main chapel in the old Hospital de las Cinco Llagas, now the headquarters of the Andalusian Parliament. He also designed Sevilla's Town Hall, the Royal Prison, the Cartuja or Charterhouse of Santa María de las Cuevas monastery. His work also included various hospitals, convents and churches, as well as the renovations to the gates in the town walls. La Giralda, named after the *giraldillo* or weather vane on the top, was built by the Moors as a minaret above their mosque. It subsequently became the bell tower for the Christian cathedral and is undoubtedly the most beautiful building in the capital city of Andalucía.

Hernán Ruiz III continued working as an architect on renovations and repairs of many of the buildings designed by his father and grandfather, but he never achieved the fame of his namesakes as a draughtsman. He inherited from his father, El Mozo, his extensive library of books relating to architecture and also hundreds of documents and plans drawn up by his grandfather El Viejo.

Included in the collection was an incomplete translation into Spanish of *De Architectvra*, the oldest known treatise on architecture in the world. Written by Marcus Vitrubius Pollio, a 1st-century Roman engineer, writer and architect, it comprises innumerable geometrical drawings, sketches of perspective, stone-cutting and carpentry, along with many architectural experiments. When it was re-edited in Rome in the late 15th century it became the quintessential reference book for Renaissance architecture throughout Europe.

The third major architect of this era is Andrés de Vandelvira, the designer of numerous monuments, palaces and churches in Andalucía. Born in 1509, he began to make a name for himself at the age of 20 as a skilful draughtsman in Uclés, in the province of Cuenca, working on the Plateresque-style convent in the town. Seven years later he landed the contract to build the Iglesia del Salvador in Úbeda together with Alonso Ruiz, following plans drawn up by Diego de Siloé.

The church, originally the chapel of a mansion belonging to Francisco de Cobos y Molina who was secretary of state to Carlos V, is unique in Spain in that it was completed in less than 20 years. More unusually, virtually no alterations have since been made. It remains to this day one of the finest examples of religious architecture in Spain.

Above the north door, Vandelvira placed a tympanum (a triangular or semi-circular decorative addition to the wall over an entrance, often containing sculptures or other ornamentation). Depicting Santiago the Moor slayer, this tympanum was to become his trademark, also being featured on the Hospital de Santiago in Úbeda and on many buildings in Baeza.

A statue of Andrés de Vandelvira, in recognition of the work he did in Úbeda, stands in its Plaza de Vázquez de Molina. By walking a mere few metres in any one direction from here, you can immerse yourself in the architecture of Spain's 'Siglo de

Oro' virtually as it was created more than 400 years ago. With every building constructed from the local yellow sandstone, the whole *plaza* glows in all its golden glory.

In the south-west corner is the old Palacio de las Cadenas, now housing the town hall, named after the chains *(cadenas)* that once decorated the façade. Opposite, just beyond the emblematic stone lions marking the south-eastern limits of the old palace grounds, is the huge church of Santa María de los Reales Alcázares. Constructed on the site of an old mosque, its façade topped by a double belfry, hides from view an elegant cloister that encloses what was the original Moorish ablutions patio.

Next to this is another stately mansion, the Palacio de Marqués de Mancera. Further on, the Antiguo Pósito, an old granary that later became the town's prison, is today the police station. On the opposite side is the Palacio del Condestable Dávalos, now a Parador. A superbly proportioned building with a spectacular arcaded interior patio, it is one of the most impressive hotels of the Parador chain in Andalucía.

All of these buildings, together with the Iglesia del Salvador, which stands guard at the north-eastern end of the Plaza de Vázquez de Molina, form part of the finest collection of Renaissance architecture in the whole of Spain.

Away from the centre of Úbeda, and outside the original walls, is the Hospital de Santiago, now used as a multi-service exhibition and conference centre. Not only is this considered Vandelvira's most mature architectural work, it is also a symbol of the city along with the Iglesia del Salvador. In comparison with the architect's earlier works, it is an austere building.

The plain walls are relieved only by beautiful brickwork and delicate tiered arcades.

Commissioned by the bishop of Jaén as a place to treat sufferers of syphilis, the huge edifice is flanked by four, high, non-identical square towers. The blue, white and yellow tiling on the turret of one tower, renovated centuries later, lends a colourful contrast to the rest of this relatively ascetic construction whose unadorned design is somewhat untypical of its time.

Andrés de Vandelvira also designed several of the palaces and mansion houses, churches and public monuments in the nearby town of Baeza. He was employed by many of the local nobility there who had become rich from the thriving textile industry of the time. Baeza is smaller and less formal than its neighbour but, like Úbeda, suffered with the collapse of the region's economy during the 17th century. From this resulted a fortunate side-effect. The town's Renaissance architectural legacy was preserved, as almost no newer large buildings were constructed for a very long time.

In the splendid Plaza de Santa María, the elevated, square structure of the cathedral was for the most part devised by Vandelvira. It overlooks a fountain almost Baroque in the extravagance of its design. Built like a triumphal arch, with ornate decoration and bearing the arms of Felipe II, the fountain stands in front of the plain façade of the old 17th-century seminary of San Felipe Neri, now housing the International University of Andalucía.

The cathedral, in common with so many religious buildings of the era, was built on the site of an old mosque. The mosque had, in turn, been constructed over an ancient pagan temple. Inside, the fine nave of the cathedral is very similar in design to that of Jaén, although on a much smaller scale.

Later in his life Vandelvira moved to Jaén where he designed his masterpiece: the Catedral de la Asunción. Since the end of the 14th century, when the old Moorish mosque was demolished on the order of the Catholic Kings, there had been a few unsuccessful attempts to build a grand Christian building in its place. Finally permission to begin construction of the cathedral was granted in 1570, five years before Vandelvira's death. It was not completed until the end of the 18th century.

To achieve a sense of its grandeur and size Jaén cathedral is best looked down on from the Santa Catalina castle that now houses the local Parador. Taking up a vast space in the centre of the city, its western façade alone is 33 metres wide and rises to 32 metres. This is without including the two identical bell-towers, one at either end, which elevate the structure by at least another 20 metres.

The construction as a whole is magnificently proportioned, with a large dome which, viewed from above, sits centrally towards the eastern end. Inside, the design is sombre compared with the exuberance of the exterior with a mass of Corinthian columns soaring to the roof of the nave. The richly carved choir stalls depict scenes from the Old Testament as well as various macabre martyrdoms. Considered the high point of Renaissance religious architecture in Spain, it formed the blueprint for a great number of churches in South America.

CULTURE IN NATURE

Ancient olive tree

Bird of paradise (strelitzia)

Introduction

The word 'culture', deriving from the Latin verb *colere*, originally signified 'to care for the land'. Its meaning has extended to many other words connected with nature, such as agri-culture (cultivating the land), horti-culture (cultivation of plants) or aqua-culture (farming of any organisms that live in water).

In 18th-century Europe the concept of culture began to signify the improvement in agricultural or horticultural methods and around a century later it was applied to the betterment of the individual through education. Culture has now become a universal description embracing all human traditions, ways of working and lifestyles typical to an area.

Living in the mountains or along river valleys, humans have sought to control nature innummerable ways, with water an ever-present factor. They originally used natural caves for shelter, and developed tools and built settlements from stones and wood, invariably settling near a mountain spring or gently flowing watercourse. When the Romans arrived in the 2nd century BC, they brought with them the technology to build wells, deposits and aqueducts. This enabled them to live farther from a source of fresh water which could then be channelled to their settlements and stored.

The Moors, during their eight-century occupation of Al-Andalus, restored and renovated many of these water features, extending and improving them for their own use. They created beautiful gardens and patios around fountains and ponds and constructed intricately tiled public baths. Their legacy of irrigation systems is still with us today in the complex network of channels and in the wells, ancient waterwheels and other hydraulic machinery functioning, even now, in parts of the region.

Although crops and fruit and vegetables need water to a greater or lesser degree, olive trees can survive many years of drought. The quality of the annual yield of olives may depend upon how much rain has fallen the previous winter, but the tree itself does not need artificial watering.

Native to Mediterranean areas, the olive tree was brought to the shores of southern Spain by Phoenician traders in the 6th century BC. Oil from the fruit has been used for cooking, heating and lighting for thousands of years. In Roman times, hundreds of hectares of land were planted with olive trees and millions of amphorae containing olives and their oil were transported back to the capital of the Imperial Empire.

A whole culture has since grown up around the cultivating and marketing of olive oil. Spain is now a world leader in the production of olives, with the industry predominating in the province of Jaén. Evidence has been discovered that wine was produced from grapes in the Middle East around 6000BC, but in Andalucía, it was the Romans, once again, who laid out the extensive viticulture foundation which continues to this day.

While some wine-growing areas, such as those around Manilva in the province of Málaga, have diminished, others that were abandoned completely have been revived using new techniques as can be seen in the Ronda area. As long as the rains come at the right time during the year, grape vines also survive for many years. Modern vineyards however often install automatic watering systems to guarantee consistency in the quality of the fruit.

The modern concept of 'culture' covers the traditions surrounding the pursuits so typical of Andalucía's natural environment. From wine making and olive production, to basket weaving and numerous other artisan activities still to be found in the eight provinces, for each and every one there is a vital ingredient – water.

Rippling shadows on water

A liquid legacy

When you fly over the arid mountain ranges of Andalucía, it is hard to imagine the vast resource lying in aquifers and natural lakes beneath the craggy, limestone outcrops and parched river valleys. But appearances can be deceptive. Explore those valleys and venture through the surrounding scrubland and you will find evidence of water in hidden springs, or the remains of ancient waterways. Early settlers made their homes near these natural springs or by the wide rivers that flowed through the region.

A cultural-historical guide, entitled *Breve Guía del Patrimonio Hidráulico de Andalucía* (Brief Guide to Andalucía's Hydraulic Heritage) has been published by the Junta de Andalucía. It highlights some of the most important monuments and architectural features built from Roman times to the 20th century, to carry, channel, contain and provide water in the eight provinces of Andalucía.

It describes the fountains and pools in Granada's Alhambra Palace, Monturque's Roman cisterns in Córdoba and the Moorish Baños del Alcázar in Jerez de la Frontera. Also featured are the flour mills in Alcalá de Guadaira (Sevilla), the Baños de la Reina in Berja (Almería) and the spectacular Caños de Carmona aqueduct in Sevilla.

During the eight centuries the Moors ruled in Al-Andalus they created some of the greatest monuments for the use of water in Europe. In Ronda, at the confluence of the Guadalevín River and the Arroyo de las Culebras, they built one of their large *hammans*. This bath-house has been very well preserved. You can walk down into what was the entrance hall before going through into the three main rooms. The central one is divided into three by pairs of horseshoe arches on brick and stone pillars supporting vaulted ceilings that are punctuated by sky-lights in the shape of stars.

The Moors brought with them age-old ways of cultivating the land. Based on their skilful methods of water management they turned many parts of Al-Andalus into an earthly paradise with lush gardens, productive crops and fruitful orchards. Near Alhaurín el Grande, in the Río Grande valley, they also built numerous flour mills. Some, like the Molino de los Corchos, still function today.

Further north near Ardales is a well-known spa, Carratraca, lying at one of the gateways to the Guadalhorce valley. The town was settled by the Moors who used the sulphur springs for curative effects. But it was not until the 19th century that the place became fashionable amongst more affluent people seeking 'to take the waters'. As a result, a new spa was built in the mid-19th century and it is still popular today.

With populations rapidly increasing, especially in the cities, damming rivers to store water became a viable option. The river Guadalhorce, after passing the town of Antequera, meanders westwards through an extensive plain where there are many natural lakes fed by other rivers flowing down the northern flanks of the Sierra de las Nieves. Where the river turns south, the Conde del Guadalhorce dam was built in the early 1900s at the head of El Chorro gorge together with a large hydro-electric plant.

El Chorro is perhaps better known for its spectacular scenery and the Caminito del Rey. This narrow, three-kilometre long path was named after Alfonso XIII who, in 1921, walked the whole length when inaugurating the dam. Built into the walls of the Desafiladero de los Gaitanes, a sheer-sided canyon gouged out by the Guadalhorce River, the path hangs precipitously 100 metres above the river and at present is in serious need of renovation.

Above these lakes and reservoirs, in the Sierra de las Nieves near Tolox and Yunquera, there are still signs of the ancient *pozos de nieve* or snow wells. By the middle of the 17th century, snow had become a very marketable commodity and Málaga city in particular, with its busy port, required large quantities.

The snow wells at Puerto de los Ventisqueros and Puerto del Cuco, 1700 metres above sea level, were in use for centuries until relatively recently when the refrigerator became a common household appliance. The *neveros*, or snow-men, used to cut the snow with large wooden spades, carrying it on their backs to the wells which were about half a metre deep and up to 10 metres in diameter. There it would be stamped down, covered with *aulaga morisca*, a gorse-like shrub, then a layer of earth, and stored until the summer when it was taken down to the towns near the coast on the backs of donkeys.

Over-population, mass consumption, misuse and pollution are some of the causes of a world-wide shortage of drinking water. One solution is to allow fresh water only for human consumption and places such as Gibraltar have gone some way to redress this by utilising sea water for certain purposes.

There are desalination plants in operation along coastal areas of Andalucía and these are effective, if expensive, and recycled water is used by the multitude of golf courses, but so far the region's liquid resource in its sierras remains untapped. Water is, however, a precious commodity and should not be taken for granted.

Ancient waterwheel in modern setting

Acueductos **and** *acequias*

In Andalucía you occasionally come across an ancient Roman aqueduct striding across a peaceful valley, or a mountain village which owes its living to a Moorish irrigation system. There are fountains in nearly every inland town. Some are surrounded by worn old lions that have been spouting fresh water from the time of the Iberians more than two thousand years ago. Water deposits, underground cisterns and ornamental pools have all played an important part of the cultural features in nature over the centuries.

As communities grew, they extended and improved the methods of channelling water to provide for their daily existence: for drinking, washing, crop irrigation and also for pleasure and beauty. Succeeding societies went to heights of ingenuity to provide their cities with water, sometimes bringing it from great distances.

The architectural creativity of the constructions to hold, move and disperse this precious commodity is still evident throughout Andalucía.

While *acueductos*, or aqueducts, brought in water mainly for urban use, *acequias*, or irrigation channels, are still used extensively in country areas. Conceived in the 6th century to take water from the Euphrates River for the magnificent hanging gardens of Babylon, the concept was originally brought to the western Mediterranean by the Romans. But their constructions were not durable, falling quickly into disrepair after they left.

Still to be seen in the Alpujarras, however, are the systems devised by the Moors during their occupation of Al-Andalus. As mentioned earlier, they took advantage of the abandoned Roman infrastructure, extending and intensifying its use, and constructed larger *acequias* to serve a complex network of smaller channels, so creating an ingenious system of water distribution to provide for the emerging agriculture.

Collecting and storing water is of prime importance in any area where river courses dry up during the long summers and this is the principal function of an *alberca* or water deposit. Still constructed in the *campo*, usually in the shape of a rectangular swimming pool but with none of the paraphernalia of pumps and filtration systems, the *albercas* are used today by all the family for keeping cool during weekends in July and August. The water is then drained off gradually during the week in the age-old way to irrigate the fruit and vegetables grown on the surrounding land. *Albercas* were also a necessary, and ornamental, feature in the patios and gardens built by the Moors in their towns and cities.

The most famous, and perhaps the largest in the region, is in the Patio de los Arrayanes at the Alhambra Palace in Granada. Dating from the 14th century, and measuring 34 metres long by 7.10 metres wide, it was at one time surrounded by myrtle shrubs (*arrayanes*), from which the patio gets its name.

Norias, or water wheels, have played an important part in the collection of water for more than two thousand years. Either constructed to take up water from a flowing river or built over a well, they were devised in what is now the Middle East: another scheme brought to Andalucía by the Romans who began to install them in mountainous areas. An original one can still be seen in the Sierra Morena to the north-west of Sevilla.

The Moors further developed these *norias* in Andalucía as most of them had fallen into disuse when the Romans left and they built others which measured more than 15 metres in diameter. Taking advantage of an area of river with increased flow, the water was collected by means of *cangilones*, or 'buckets'. These were built on the wheel which, when reaching the highest point, poured the water into a main channel that fed the *acequias*, for irrigation of the land, or the *acueductos* to carry it into the towns.

An ancient Moorish *noria*, with earthenware pitchers strapped to the wheel, instead of the wooden or metal 'buckets', can be seen in the Parque María Cristina in the centre of Algeciras. But for an example of large water wheel built in the 18th century, there is one on the Río Genil near Córdoba which was used in conjunction with a flour mill.

Besides providing for basic essentials to feed their growing populations, succeeding civilisations which conquered and settled in southern Spain left behind many examples of their baths and spas. Established where water sprang naturally from the ground, there are magnificent examples of Moorish and Roman baths in Ronda, Jaén and Málaga, as well as many other places in Andalucía. One of the most intriguing, Las Bóvedas, is in Guadalmina, near San Pedro Alcántara.

Built in the 3rd century, and possibly used by the Romans as thermal baths, they were only discovered in 1926, having been buried under the sands of time as the sea level rose and fell. They were constructed around an octagonal vaulted patio of more than nine metres in diameter, and parallel to its walls are signs of an *alberca* 1.20 metres deep. The upper floor consisted of a circular gallery giving access to small rooms. Today, having been conserved and partially reconstructed, Las Bóvedas is the occasional venue for open-air summer concerts.

Healing sulphur springs bubble up at the Baños de Hedionda near Manilva. Cloudy, foul smelling water maybe, but said to be good for many skin complaints. In Roman times the river was navigable up to this point and legend has it that Caesar stopped here during his conquering campaign of the Iberian Peninsula, seeking to cure his eczema, and subsequently ordering the baths to be constructed.

The baths are still in use, freely available to those who go down the narrow, worn, old stone steps. They provide the only way into the water and if you want to see the main chamber, for most of the year, you have to swim virtually underwater to reach it. But once there in the cool and peaceful interior you can soak up not only the sulphur, but an atmosphere of a long-forgotten culture.

Now half submerged underground, the original building was in the form of a simple square, with sides measuring about six metres, and having a spherical, vaulted ceiling. Subsequent remodelling was at the hands of the Moors and it was they who built the outer walls and a system of channels to take the spring water outside.

The Romans were extravagant in the magnitude of many of their buildings designed to contain and to use water and the Moors decorated theirs profusely. These influences still appear in modern-day swimming pools: the Roman design of long, simple rectangles with three straight sides and the fourth rounded with shallow steps going down into the water; the Moorish décor with geometric borders and mosaic tiles. And we continue also to enjoy the legacy of Al-Andalus in the colourfully decorated water features set in palatial patios and luxuriant gardens of most towns and cities in Andalucía.

One of the earliest examples of an ornamental construction surrounding a water source is the Fuente de los Leones in Baeza, near Úbeda on the northern flank of the Guadalquivir valley. Claimed to be Iberian in origin, the ancient fountain is guarded by stone lions whose features have almost disappeared over the centuries.

But fountains are found everywhere, an essential part of towns and villages throughout the region. Some are of simple design, a mere stone or metal pipe protruding from a wall to supply drinking water to a mountainside community, or the classic trough with three or five spouts in the historic centres of many towns. Others are extravagantly built and lavishly decorated. In all of them, the sound and sight of the water brings a sense of peace.

Jardines Botánicos de la Concepción, Málaga

In the gardens of Andalucía

The play of water on stone or tile is essential to a garden in Andalucía. The style of modern gardens, providing light and shade, colour and greenery, is a continuation of designs that have been used down the centuries. Spiritual and ornamental aspects became more widely developed during Moorish times and gardens began to include fountains and pools with elaborate mosaic designs. They also featured neatly arrayed trees, clipped evergreen hedges, aromatic flowers and herbs.

Fashioned around rulers' palaces, or the mansions of affluent families, gardens became not only an ornamental extension of the living quarters, they were also somewhere to find peace and tranquillity. The gardens of the Generalife close to the Alhambra Palace in Granada, created between the 12th and 14th centuries, are a classic example of the way the Moors blended architecture, formal gardens and orchards in perfect harmony. The sound of water is always present; trickling into ponds, spurting up in fountains or gurgling along channels beside the pathways.

The Jardines de los Reales Alcázares in Sevilla, originally laid out in the 10th century by Abd al-Rahman II, now cover an area of 60,000 square metres and contain more than 170 species of plants and trees. While in Córdoba, the Jardines del Conde de Vallellano, which were originally built around a 1st-century Roman water deposit, have an extensive variety of trees and shrubs. Today the gardens accommodate a large, more modern 'pond' containing more than 3000 cubic metres of water.

There are municipal parks and gardens in all the major towns and cities of Andalucía. Along the Paseo del Parque in Málaga, on land reclaimed from the sea, is a subtropical, botanical garden boasting more than 150 different species of trees and shrubs. To the north of the city lies the English-style garden of La Concepción. Created in the mid 19th century, there are more than 5000 examples of plant life including around 500 tropical and subtropical species, as well as numerous different types of palm tree.

Many of the fruits growing in private or public gardens in Andalucía today were brought here many centuries ago. The pomegranate, grown by ancient cultures for its medicinal properties and known to have been cultivated for at least 5000 years in western Asia, was brought by the Berbers from northern Africa. It has appeared on the national coat of arms of Spain since the 15th century when the Catholic Kings added it following their conquest of the city of Granada. The word *granada* means pomegranate in Spanish.

The fig, of which today there are more than 700 different species worldwide, is another fruit tree that can be found in the majority of gardens and *fincas* in the region. Figs have been grown in the Jordan Valley since before 9000BC and evidence of the fruit has also been found in excavation sites in Turkey dating from 5000BC. Considered by the Moors as a symbol of fecundity, it was first brought to Andalucía by the Romans and has been widely cultivated ever since. Some varieties bear two annual crops. The tree first produces the *breva*, a larger fruit than the sweeter *higo* which ripens a few months later and comprises the main crop.

Another ancient fruit is the *aceituna*, or olive, known to have been grown in Andalucía 8000 years ago. The tree, which also graces numerous gardens, can be seen nowadays in its millions marching in neat rows throughout the hinterland, especially in the provinces of Jaén, Granada and Córdoba. Its branch is the symbol of peace and the oil from its fruit, rich in vitamin E, is probably found in every kitchen throughout Spain.

Innumerable poems have been written, music has been composed and lyrics compiled extolling the splendour, the values and the appeal of gardens. But perhaps one of the best known works relating specifically to Andalucía is by the Spanish composer, Manuel de Falla (1876–1946). *Nights in the Gardens of Spain* was inspired by three different gardens. The first movement evokes the jasmine-scented gardens of the Generalife in Granada, the Jannat al-Arif or architect's garden, one of the oldest surviving Moorish gardens. The origin of the second is unidentified, but from its gypsy melodies is probably somewhere in Sevilla. The third movement depicts the gardens at Madinat al-Zahra, in the Sierra de Córdoba.

Construction of the gardens at Medina Azahara, as this town is now known, began in the year 936 by Abd al-Rahman III and continued under the guardianship of his son. Taking advantage of the slope of the land, the palace of these Arab caliphs was built on various levels and so commanded extensive views from all the principal rooms.

The ornate ceremonial salon led out on to the substantial *Jardín Alto* or High Garden, in whose centre was a square pavilion surrounded on each side by long rectangular pools. The largest of these pools, on the north side, reflected the sumptuous décor of the palace's Salón Rico, a spectacular effect which was duplicated by the pavilion itself built in the same style.

The garden was on a platform reinforced by buttresses, an idea brought from the Middle East and again reminiscent of the Hanging Gardens of Babylon. There was a second large garden on a lower level, the *Jardín Bajo*. Both were laid out with a pathway around the perimeter and two more paths that crossed each other dividing the whole into four parts. This design, with its geometrically-shaped water features and aromatic flowers, was to be much repeated in Al-Andalus.

Other gardens created by the Arabs were also used in more practical ways. One of the first botanical gardens of Al-Andalus was at Al Buhayra, the principal residence of Abu Ya'qub Usuf, the Almohad emir. Having been instrumental in the building of the bridge from the centre of Sevilla to the neighbouring district of Triana, he constructed his palace outside the city walls on the banks of the river Tagarete surrounding it with greenery, flowers and orchards. The Palacio de la Albufera, as it is known today, was a place where agriculturists and botanists worked to lay out the extensive plantations of myriad species of plants and vegetables, flowering and fruit trees.

The Moors created tranquil oases during their long occupation of Al-Andalus. Renaissance Christian kings laid out formal gardens surrounding their castles and subsequently wealthy land-owners brought back samples from their world travels to stock their estates. The late-18th century emissaries from botanical gardens went to many parts of the world on plant-collecting expeditions, subsequently publishing their findings in journals and pamphlets.

Work was then carried out to see how alien exotic species could grow in another environment and how they could be propagated before being classified for scientific purposes.

More recently, the Grice-Hutchinson Experimental Centre was set up in Málaga. It is named after Marjorie Grice-Hutchinson, an English-born economist, who died in 2003 aged 94. She came to Málaga in 1924, when her father acquired property in San Julián near the present airport, and married Baron von Schlippenbach, an agricultural engineer living and working in the area.

The botanical garden created at Finca San Julián was eventually donated by Marjorie to Málaga University. Under the auspices of UNESCO and other international organisations, the work undertaken there is part of the 'world strategy for conservation'. The idea is to develop specific conservation projects relating to the biodiversity of vegetation so as to nurture endemic species and save endangered ones.

In Churriana, just outside Málaga, Santo Tomás del Monte, a 17th-century bishop of Málaga, took over an old house and surrounded it with gardens and orchards to grow fruit and vegetables for the Dominican monks. Also used as a place for them to retire to for peace and meditation, it became known as El Retiro.

Subsequent owners added to the collection of plants and trees, but it fell into disuse in the 20th century. A crumbly and romantic place to visit, with dark evergreens, old marble statues and trickling fountains greened over with time, it has today become a more commercial venture with a large ornithological centre. But you can still lose yourself along the winding paths that thread their way through exotic vegetation, or find a peaceful corner to sit and contemplate the faded grandeur to the sound of water.

Moorish and Christian towers, Olvera

Vía Verde de la Sierra

No train has ever passed along the thirty-six kilometres of rail track known today as the Vía Verde de la Sierra. One of the most southerly of the *vías verdes* or 'green routes' in Spain, it is part of an extensive network that has been transformed into paths for walkers, cyclists and horse riders. Individual associations and foundations, responsible for the maintenance and upkeep of the *vías verdes*, have been set up to promote rural tourism along the routes and to develop economic activities for the villages in each respective area.

Some of these *vías* are less than five kilometres long, others more than seventy. The majority have been remodelled or even asphalted, but many are as they used to be when the trains ran and some still have the original railway lines in place. There are around 7000 kilometres of these deserted railway tracks throughout the country. Many have to date been adopted officially by the Department of the Environment to form these rural pathways.

The Vía Verde de la Sierra was originally planned as a rail link from Jerez de la Frontera to Almargen, where it would have then connected up with the route still in operation that goes on to Campillos and Antequera. Construction started at the beginning of the 20th century, having been eagerly awaited by generations of *gaditanos* and *sevillanos*, in the provinces of Cádiz and Sevilla, and also by the military who wanted a direct rail connection between their bases at Cádiz and Cartagena.

During the mid-twenties and early thirties work on the track was accelerated under the orders of General Primo de Rivera, himself a *jerezano*, to the extent that everything was in place apart from laying the railway lines themselves. With the onset of the Spanish Civil War in 1936 it all stopped. Thereafter the political and economic climate did not favour improvements in the infrastructure throughout most of Andalucía. The whole project was shelved completely in the 1960s, leaving a legacy of viaducts, tunnels and abandoned station buildings.

Running between Puerto Serrano and Olvera, the Vía Verde de la Sierra passes five stations, goes over four viaducts and through 30 tunnels, meandering gently uphill from 150 to 450 metres above sea level. But you do not need to be a serious climber or a mountain goat to follow this green pathway. For the most part the gradients are quite gentle.

At one end of the *vía* is the old station building at Puerto Serrano, now housing a small hotel and restaurant. This small, peaceful town, on the Sevilla-Cádiz provincial border just to the north of the Grazalema Natural Park, lies near the banks of the Guadalete. It was an important river in olden times as it was navigable from El Puerto de Santa María up to this point.

Due to its geographical situation in a particularly fertile river valley, the area has been settled for thousands of years, with archaeological findings proving the existence of humans from Neolithic and Paleolithic eras. Remains, dating from the 2nd century BC, have also been uncovered of a necropolis, or burial place, in the form of caves hewn out of the rocks. Roman mosaics and red marble columns from 100BC that were found in the region can now be seen in the Archaeological Museum in Sevilla.

The only deviation from the route of the original railway track comes not far from Puerto Serrano at a tunnel named El Indiano after the ancient *finca* upon which it was originally constructed. So many landslides occurred inside this tunnel after it was built in the nineteen thirties that reconstruction has not been feasible, so the Vía Verde de la Sierra makes its way around the outside.

A few kilometres further on, after emerging from the tunnel of Los Azares, named perhaps after the short but spectacular track that clings precariously to the mountainside over the Río Guadalete, where you 'take your chance', the *vía* goes through one that is well preserved and runs for 500 metres. Although lit throughout, you are advised to take your own torch, just in case … of what? … of power cuts, bats, ghosts? Who knows? But this is not the longest of the 30 tunnels. There is another, nearly one kilometre in length, immediately after Junta de los Ríos where the *vía* leaves the river it has been running alongside and begins to follow the Río Guadalporcún.

A short viaduct crosses the Arroyo de Gillete, the quaintly named 'Razor Blade Stream', and then a longer one leads the walker or rider into Coripe station, remodelled to house a small hotel and restaurant. In common with many railway stations in Andalucía, it is so far from the town from which it gets it name that gradually a settlement grew up around it. So as well as the town of Coripe, we have also have that of Estación de Coripe.

From here to Zaframagón there are five more tunnels. The Peñón de Zaframagón, a rocky, limestone outcrop more than 580 metres high, is home to one of the most important colonies of griffon vultures in Europe. A camera with a powerful zoom lens has been set up at the Interpretation Centre, in the reconstructed Zaframagón station, for people to watch these noble birds without disturbing them. The images, projected on to a large screen for viewing at the centre, are all saved and used by environment professionals to study the numbers and habits of the vultures.

After crossing the elegant Zaframagón viaduct which rises high above the Río Guadalporcún, the *vía* goes under the Peñón and emerges some 700 metres later into a very different type of terrain. With the jagged outlines of the distant Sierra de Líjar silhouetted against the sky, the track winds its way through undulating grasslands, past livestock grazing on large farms on either side to come into Estación de Navalagrulla. This is the last station before Olvera. The *vía* then rises steadily upwards on the final stretch through pale green olive groves, gently gaining nearly 100 metres in altitude over five kilometres.

The station at Olvera, perhaps the most beautiful railway building of the Vía Verde de la Sierra, has also been converted into a hotel and restaurant. Not only is it a delightful place to stay at the start or end of your journey, it provides a good base from which to explore the surrounding countryside. The town of Olvera, standing proudly on a massive, high, rocky outcrop, is at the crossroads of many routes between the provinces of Cádiz, Málaga and Sevilla.

When approaching from Algodonales, the view of the town could not be more dramatic, with white-washed houses clinging to the steep slopes and the towers of the Moorish castle and Catholic church standing sentinel at the top. The Moors settled here at the end of the 12th century and built a small fortress and watchtower that formed part of the far-reaching defensive system of the Nasrid kingdom of Granada. In the 15th century, following the Christian *reconquista*, the Catholics constructed a large church over part of the Moorish structure. The building that can be seen today, the church of Nuestra Señora de la Encarnación, dates however from the 19th century.

The fact that the green pathways often follow a relatively level course is one of the attractions for ramblers, and of great importance for the physically impaired who can also enjoy them. All the stations are easily accessible by car, so you can choose to explore shorter or longer parts of the route. Far away from any roads or houses, the *vías* go through unspoilt countryside, virgin forests and spectacular mountain landscapes. They give the walker and rider a unique chance to savour the peace and tranquillity of our natural environment.

CULTURAL FUSION

Girl's flamenco dress

Palacio de la Aduana (under wraps), Málaga

Introduction

Layer upon layer of styles, of civilisations, of customs and traditions: each takes something from the last and merges it with the present. Excavations for new buildings or roads uncover a wealth of information and treasures of the past. Much of the old, belonging to different peoples or different cultures, is preserved and put on public display in modern purpose-built centres. Books are written about the findings to inform the present multi-national generations of times gone by. Photographs are taken; art forms mix and merge once again to form a separate medium or a fusion of media.

The supreme example of cultural fusion in Andalucía, not only of architectural styles but also of religions, is the Grand Mosque in Córdoba which envelops a Catholic cathedral. Another example, although transitory, was seen in Málaga's Plaza de la Merced. The six-storey frontage of what is now home to the Picasso Foundation was protected for many months by a *trompe l'oeil* cloth. On it was a painting of a façade from another era; an ingenious way of concealing dusty building work and a work of art in its own right.

Subsequently the same style of device was used around the whole of the large Palacio de la Aduana (see photograph on previous page). This 19th-century, Neo-Classic building, originally destined to deal with customs and port administration, is now the site of the city's Fine Arts Museum.

Music and dance, literature and the theatre, they all blend and overlap. Film director Carlos Saura's 2005 documentary *Iberia* is a fusion of flamenco music with the musical suite of the same name composed by Isaac Albéniz. Contemporary flamenco combines with traditional Spanish dance. Sara Baras, one of the film's protagonists, dances sublimely as she has danced in innumerable shows of her own, interpreting roles such as Mariana Pineda, the heroine of a play written by Federico García Lorca. Sounds, movement and words, with flamenco pervading it all. The life blood of Andalucía is sensed, experienced and performed with *duende* – the spirit, the magic and the mystery of the region.

With roots hidden in those of the mixed society of the region, flamenco was appropriated by the gypsy race that came here from Africa and from central and eastern Europe. Arab melodies, Middle Eastern harmony and Jewish modal tones are now being merged with American jazz, Cuban salsa and Argentinean tango. It is a fusion of cultures which in themselves are a fusion of older cultures.

Gran Teatro Falla, Cádiz

Following flamenco routes

Flamenco has gradually been taken out from back street bars of Cádiz and Sevilla and the caves of Granada to be turned into a musical art form in its own right. From the sometime solitary and spontaneous outpouring of passionate song, today's sophisticated and spectacular shows performed in front of thousands, flamenco can now be seen and heard at venues all over the world, including the well known international theatres of New York's Lincoln Center or London's Festival Hall.

Although its origins are obscure, flamenco roots can be found in the multi-cultural music of Al-Andalus. Many of the lyrics still reflect the turbulent times at the end of that era when Moors, Gypsies and Jews were expelled from their homeland during the Christian *Reconquista*. And it is the *gitanos*, the gypsies, who have been, and still are, fundamental in maintaining this musical genre. It is part of their culture, with folk songs passed down orally through the generations by repeated performances within their social community. Most of the best known flamenco artists today, especially the singers, are mainly of gypsy origin.

Flamenco initially consisted of unaccompanied singing *(cante)*. The songs were later complemented by the guitar *(toque)* and the percussion box *(cajón)*, as well as rhythmic hand clapping *(palmas)*, feet stamping *(zapateado)* and then dance *(baile)*. The complex structure of flamenco is made up of as many as 50 different *palos* or styles, each distinguished by its own recurring beat or rhythm, the *compás*. For example, *cante jondo*, or deep song, the very foundation of flamenco, consists of 12 beats, accentuated on the third and then the sixth, eighth, tenth and twelfth.

Some of the dances and the songs are, by tradition, performed separately by the men or by the women. But as even the strict social codes of the gypsy race are softening, so these constraints are gradually being broken down in flamenco music. The *farruca*, formerly the exclusive preserve of the male dancer, is now performed by both sexes.

In every genre of music, there are rules, but in flamenco there exists enormous scope to improvise. Each act, each interplay between the performers, is challenging, exhilarating and physically stimulating, with the guitarist or percussionist rigorously attentive to the singer or dancer.

The so-called 'golden age' of flamenco spanned nearly half a century from the 1860s. Many *cafés cantantes*, where flamenco music was sung and played, sprang up in cities of Andalucía. One of the most famous in Málaga, the Café de Chinitas, later became a meeting place in the 1920s and 1930s for celebrated artists and writers. It was immortalised in a poem by Federico

García Lorca. Lorca, together with composer Manuel de Falla and classic guitarist Andrés Segovia, were instrumental in organising one of the first singing competitions in the city. This was won by a young gypsy boy who had walked all the way from Jerez de la Frontera to participate. Manolo Caracol went on to become a legend in his lifetime throughout Spain and also in South America.

Modern flamenco has enveloped other musical genres such as jazz, pop and rock, or rumba and salsa. It is this fusion that has perhaps made it more acceptable to a wider audience, in particular to those who have never experienced the sound of Andalucía *in situ*. But purists are still enthused by the original form and virtually every town in southern Spain has its own *peña flamenca* or flamenco club.

Festivals and annual competitions abound. One of the oldest is the Cante de las Minas International Festival, held every year in the town of La Unión, just over the eastern border of Andalucía in the province of Murcia. The original idea stemmed from a local singing competition. Not only was this to find new flamenco talent but, more importantly, to ensure the continuance of its popularity which was waning almost to the point of extinction under a regime that considered it a 'bad influence' on the people. Celebrating its 50th anniversary in 2010, the festival is the mecca to which aspiring young flamenco artists gravitate with hope and enthusiasm and from where they go on to seek out national and international fame.

Many other festivals, such as the Bienal de Flamenco in Sevilla, have gained national importance over recent decades. But the one in Murcia stands out from the rest for many reasons, not least the high financial awards for the winners. The manner in which the selection of participating *cantaores*, the flamenco singers, is organised is also significant. Instead of marathon sessions over one or more days at the festival itself, numerous elimination rounds are held in local *peñas* throughout the region and beyond in the months running up to the big event. The semi-finals, open to the public free of charge, and the grand finals are events eagerly awaited each year in La Unión.

In the province of Cádiz, there are on average more than 30 major flamenco festivals annually. These mainly occur in the month of August, with events in Algeciras and Jerez de la Frontera, as well Sanlúcar de Barrameda, El Bosque, Castellar de la Frontera, Chipiona, Rota and Arcos de la Frontera. And in Málaga province there are public flamenco performances in Ojén, Ronda, Estepona, Torremolinos and Mijas, along with many other towns. Granada's most emblematic festival is the Noche de Flamenco del Albaicín.

Savouring the sound and sight of flamenco is a moving experience. But to do so in Andalucía, the cradle of this musical art form, is unforgettable. Whether in a cave near Granada, a local *peña* or club in Málaga, a *tablao* or show in Sevilla, or in the Gran Teatro Falla in Cádiz, the rhythm and beat, colour and movement all merge into a poignant memory that stays with you long after the performance is over.

Flamenco is one of the most attractive tourist resources of southern Spain and is being increasingly promoted by the Junta de Andalucía. Routes are organised to take people on themed tours around the region. They are held in places of historic and traditional interest, such as palaces, wine cellars, vineyards, ancient hotels and country mansions. This offers an opportunity to combine learning about flamenco with soaking up the incomparable cultural atmosphere of the region. The routes are aimed to help everyone get to know and appreciate flamenco in its own surroundings. Distinguishing one style from another and finding out about its history, its traditions and how it has evolved are all explained. Details are given about the basic *palos*, or styles of flamenco, with clarification on how to differentiate between one and the other and on their various characteristics.

These routes have been designed in collaboration with the Agencia Andaluza del Flamenco, an organisation based in Sevilla. Responsible for developing and co-ordinating all policies relating to flamenco, it focuses on conservation for posterity and dissemination to the world at large.

One of the principle aims of the agency is to integrate flamenco fully into the musical market. It does this by establishing and consolidating it as a cultural industry and promoting flamenco not only in Andalucía but throughout Spain, Europe and worldwide.

The focus of these routes centres on some of the great flamenco singers who have travelled through the region and performed to audiences in venues large and small. José Monge Cruz, otherwise known as Camarón de la Isla, the legend of San Fernando (Cádiz), died aged 42 at the height of his fame. Calixto Sánchez who, after a successful career, became a director of the Centro Andaluz de Flamenco. Antonio Mairena who gave his name to the Casa del Arte Flamenco in his home town of Mairena del Alcor (Sevilla). Enrique Morente from Granada, a controversial contemporary singer-songwriter who alternated tradition with innovation. The list of names of the great is seemingly endless.

One route, entitled Ruta de Cayetano, evokes the memory of Cayetano Muriel Reyes, known throughout the flamenco world as El Niño de Cabra (the boy from Cabra). Born in the town of Cabra in 1870, he gave up his job at the mill when he was twenty to travel all around Andalucía and much of Spain, singing in cafés and at flamenco shows. He made more than 90 recordings before his death in 1947 and is still considered one of the best interpreters of the fandango.

This latter route begins in Puente Genil, the birthplace of Antonio Fernández Díaz, known artistically as Fosforito, and a visit to the *peña flamenco*, or flamenco association, established in his name is on the schedule. Born in 1932 and although not of the gypsy race, Fosforito has gained the love and admiration of his peers and the general public. In 2005 he was awarded the prestigious *Llave de Oro del Cante* (Golden Key of Song) for dignifying and popularising flamenco, for his absolute dominance of all its forms and his continuous work in reviving abandoned styles.

The *verdiales*, a type of folkloric singing and dancing, found mainly in the Axarquía region and around Almogía and the Montes de Málaga, are also included. Considered to be the precursor of the Málaga fandango, and therefore an important part of the flamenco scene, the *verdiales* have scarcely evolved. They retain their primitive style of song, handed down through the generations, and their original musical instruments and colourful costumes.

The spotlight turns occasionally to the *bajañi*, sometimes called the *bajandí*, the name given to the guitar in Romany *caló* or jargon. *Caló*, a mixed language spoken by Spanish gypsies, has a grammatical Spanish base with variable Romany gypsy vocabulary. Documented since the early 18th century, together with Portuguese-Brasilian *calâo*, Catalan *romanó* and the Basque *errumantxela*, it formed the Iberian variation of the Romany language. When coming into contact with the Castilian Spanish or the Catalan vernacular it fractured into dialects and then into what is now known as neo-Romany.

Finally, the *cantes básicos* or basic song forms. Flamenco music styles are classified into *palos*. They are based musically on rhythmic patterns, progression of chords and stanzas, and as well on geographic origin. Within these *palos* there are also variations, as for example with the tango, one of the basic styles of flamenco. Usually with three or four, eight-syllable verses, the most popular originate from Cádiz, Triana, Jerez de la Frontera and Málaga.

Tango, originally a fusion of various forms of music taken to Argentina by European emigrants, became hugely popular as a dance in the early 1900s. It has now found its way back to Andalucía in dance and song form to merge with the so-called 'pure' flamenco of the region and so create yet another musical genre.

Flamenco guitar

Communication in language and music

Communication between people has taken many forms over the centuries. Simple systems of making marks on stone, wood, clay or papyrus were used as a primitive language for passing on an order or a warning, as were bonfires lit on hilltops, and shells were used as foghorns. The triton trumpet shell *(charonia tritonis)*, with its very large opening, makes a wonderful amplifier. When blown by someone with extra-strong lungs the low, loud sound can be heard over extraordinary distances and quite complicated messages could be conveyed from village to village. In fact, any conch or shell can be used to make music by drilling a hole in it. The sound produced depends upon the size of the hole and the type of shell.

In more remote parts of the hinterland of Andalucía, a farmer working his fields can still occasionally be heard breaking into song, to a tune which would have been familiar to his great-grandfathers. The clear sounds carry easily on a still day as he greets a neighbour on the other side of the valley.

The bells around the necks of the goats munching their way over the hillsides make their own distinctive music. As the animals follow one another, the tone of the leader's bell tells every member of the herd where to go. Primitive modes of communication maybe, but still effective.

In the Middle Ages, culture and communication in Spain developed in two separate directions. The northern regions maintained close contact with European customs and traditions, mainly as a result of the hundreds of pilgrims arriving to walk the Camino de Santiago from the French border to Compostela. The early epic poems, which had originated in Provence in southern France, blended with troubadour melodies and lyrics and were sung and acted out all along the route. Adapted to *gallego*, the language of Galicia, these popular minstrel verses then appeared as a clerical verse form, or plain chant, and developed into the traditional *coplas*, or couplets, of that part of the country.

In contrast, the south was influenced by the continuing Moorish presence. Andalucía, an important international centre of Islamic culture, assimilated much of the Arab language and its music. After the *reconquista*, there emerged a fusion of the three dominant cultures: Moorish, Jewish and Christian. Their harmonisation and cultural exchanges, providing at that time one of the most fruitful periods in European culture, are still apparent today.

Music, always an integral part of the culture of Andalucía, communicates different feelings to different people. During Semana Santa, or Easter Week, an important feature of the solemn processions that wind through the streets of every town and village is the *saeta*. Dating from the 18th century, it was in the early 1900s that the original songs encouraging devotion and penitence merged with profound sentiments of a more secular nature.

Expressed by the *cante flamenco, saetas* communicate their message to believers. But you do not have to be *andaluz*, or of the Catholic faith, to experience that overwhelming frisson on hearing one. At various points along the route of a Semana Santa procession, the *costaleros* come to a halt setting down their float carefully in the street and from an unseen balcony above the powerful and passionate tones of a *saeta* pierce the darkness and the silence of the Viernes Santo night.

Ancient writing tool

Links with the written word

From etching on cave walls and stone tablets, to scratching on parchment, the quill gave way to the fountain pen which in turn was set aside for the more convenient ballpoint. Until quite recently children used to be taught the italic script with its thin upstrokes, broad down strokes and elegant curls. Calligraphy, or the 'art of beautiful handwriting', with its careful formation of letters joined up artistically and laid out on a page to be pleasing to the eye, is now carried out only by *aficionados* of the craft.

Ancient, faded lettering adorns the top of the tower of 10th-century Castillo de San Marcos in El Puerto de Santa María and there are walls in Antequera that are covered with old writing. The Moors used script as a form of decoration on much of the stonework in their buildings, especially in the Alhambra at Granada.

The Romans before them left a legacy of lettering carved on the bases of temple columns, in particular at Baelo Claudia near Cádiz. But dating back to pre-history are the painted and engraved characters found in the Cueva de la Pileta at Benaoján, near Ronda.

Examples of *arte rupestre*, rock art or cave paintings, have been found in many places in Andalucía. Rough outlines of animals were scratched on the rock by hunter-gatherers using a stone, stick or animal horn. Subsequently, in the post-Palaeolithic era, ten to twenty thousand years ago, more detailed and rounded figures were drawn, along with abstract geometrical symbols and shapes of water craft complete with oars.

These outlines of animals and people evolved during the Bronze and Iron Ages into more abstract signs. They became a type of 'writing' which was then developed as a method of communication. Were it not for the arrival of the Phoenicians from the eastern Mediterranean, it might possibly have developed into a language of its own. However this 'writing' of the local Tartessians merged with that of the Phoenicians for the purposes of trade between the two areas. When the Romans invaded Andalucía, Latin was imperiously imposed and its alphabet became the basis for Spanish, as it did for other western European languages.

The most famous *arte rupestre* in Spain was chanced upon towards the end of the 19th century in the Altamira caves at Santillana del Mar (Cantabria). In 1985, they were designated a World Heritage site by UNESCO. Other rock art was discovered in the 20th century in Andalucía, notably in the area of Campo de Gibraltar and also in the Parque de los Alcornocales and around La Janda lagoon a little further to the west. Of particular interest too, especially for their intricate details, are the horses etched into the rock walls of the Cueva del Moro near Tarifa.

Now considered the most significant group of cave paintings in Europe, in 1998 the *arte rupestre* of western Andalucía was also included on the UNESCO heritage list.

Throughout the centuries, subsequent invaders and settlers in Andalucía have added their cultural expression to the area with their own form of 'writing on the wall', or graffiti. Among the most noteworthy to have survived is the Arab calligraphy etched on the stonework of the Alhambra. Tributes to the building and its builders, along with eulogies of several sultans, can be found among innumerable verses and sayings from the Koran. And repeated endlessly on the elegant arches and exquisite filigree stonework is the phrase *Wa-la ghaliba illa-Llah* – "There is no conqueror but God."

The term 'graffiti' is derived from the Greek word meaning 'to write' and the Italian meaning 'to scratch'. It signifies the drawing or writing done, almost exclusively, on a wall or other constructed surface. The singular form 'graffito' has faded into obscurity, used now only by art historians to describe the way a design is etched onto a surface.

In the sense of scratching on a surface, graffiti had already existed for tens of thousands of years. When we think of graffiti today however, what usually springs to mind is the modern leisure activity of youths running around with aerosol cans idly defacing ancient monuments and street furniture. Their message "I woz ere" appears to be the only result, or purpose, of such exploits.

In 2007, graffiti achieved official recognition in Granada at Calle Sócrates in the city centre. Four young artists from different parts of Spain were commissioned to decorate the inside walls of a newly-constructed car park. The first level is predominantly green, representing forests and lush valleys and inspired by the Greek philosopher after whom the street is named. This initiative, the first in Spain at that time, included plans to decorate the other three storeys: blue for a sea and sky theme; a minimalist spirit portrayed in reds; and finally yellow for the upper floor, symbolising the desert, the light and the sun.

Graffiti competitions and workshops are now held throughout Andalucía. The Department for Youth of the Junta de Andalucía, and of many towns and cities, also organise permanent and temporary outdoor exhibitions. In Sevilla one art gallery not only holds an annual show of works by the best graffiti artists, it also stocks materials a *grafitero* might need for his or her urban art.

In the proper place, graffiti is a genre of art in its own right, an artistic social and political expression as old as mankind. At first glance each work appears superficial. Without doubt it *is* superficial in the sense that it is drawn, painted or scratched on a surface, but usually there is an underlying message.

CULTURAL TRADITIONS

Traditional rush baskets

National emblem

Introduction

The culture and traditions of Andalucía have evolved through many different societies mixing and merging over the centuries. Not surprisingly, throughout the eight provinces of the region these traditions vary considerably.

Some echo past civilisations, with Phoenician, Roman or Moorish influences still to be found, but the strongest reflect the *reconquista*: the re-conquering of the area by the Catholic Kings. The passion with which the Christian population embraced its revival 500 years ago is still evident in the enthusiasm which goes into the many processions held throughout the year.

While Semana Santa is a fixture on everyone's calendar, and the arrival on 5th January of the *Reyes Magos*, or Three Kings, is awaited with bated breath by children everywhere, provincial capitals also have celebrations of their own. Almost every town and village holds an annual fair, as well as a fiesta in honour of its patron saint. In addition, there other festivities unique to each, including days promoting the delights of local gastronomy or festivals of music or dance.

The cultural year in Granada begins with the Fiesta de la Toma de Granada. This festival celebrates the taking of the city in 1492 by the Catholic Kings, a significant moment in the Christian re-conquest after nearly eight centuries of Moorish occupation. Held on 2nd January, the fiesta is a day of revelry and solemn parades, of parties and formal proclamations.

After mass in the cathedral, town dignitaries visit the tomb of Isabel and Ferdinand in the Royal Chapel. Processions then move through the city centre to the town hall to hoist the flag of Castile, a symbol at the time of the united Kingdom of Spain. Later in the day, unmarried girls climb up the Cerro de la Sabika, the hill on which the Alhambra is situated, to ring the bell in the Torre de la Vela. Tradition states that those who do so will be married within the year.

In late February or early March, just prior to Lent, it is carnival time in Cádiz. Perhaps the most entertaining and colourful in Europe, the Carnaval de Cádiz is second only to Río de Janeiro in the sheer vitality and enthusiasm displayed in the streets and plazas of the old city. Although carnival possibly derives from age-old bacchanalian and saturnalian orgies, its origin in Cádiz has been documented from the 16th century, a time when commerce with Italy was prospering.

The masks, streamers and confetti used to this day are just some of the elements brought to Spanish shores by Genoan traders. Masks were prohibited on various occasions during the mid 18th century and in 1816 the whole carnival was banned, though not with much success. In the late 19th century, what had been a series of disorganised fiestas was brought together in four different categories. The *chirigotas*, or satirical songs, are perhaps the most popular with the people of Cádiz.

Málaga is renowned for its Semana Santa. Thousands of people flock to the city to watch or take part in the processions which wend their way through the streets every day from *Domingo de Ramos* (Palm Sunday) to *Domingo de la Resurrección* (Easter Sunday), except for the Saturday when all is quiet. A tradition unique to Málaga is the release of a prisoner from jail on the Wednesday of Easter Week.

The custom dates back to the mid 18th century: one year, so many men had died of the plague there were not enough *costaleros*, or bearers, to carry the float of the brotherhood of 'El Rico'. Convicts were let out to fulfil this duty. In recognition of the fact they all returned voluntarily to jail after the procession had ended, Carlos III signed a Royal Decree to liberate one prisoner every year; a tradition that continues to this day.

The springtime fair in Sevilla dates back to the mid-13th century when permission was given for two annual fairs in the city, the other being in the autumn. Five centuries later the Feria de Abril, usually held two weeks after Easter, received the royal stamp of approval and ever since has gone from strength to strength.

Every year ideas are more imaginative and processions more vibrant. All the 'streets' of the fairground are named after famous bullfighters and, except for emergency services, the only form of transport in and around the extensive enclosure is by horse and carriage. The main area of entertainment, commonly known as the 'Calle del Infierno', or Street of Hell, has more than 400 attractions and rides, with such fanciful names as the *gusano loco* (mad worm), the *látigo* (whip) or the *ratón vacilón* (clown rat).

In Huelva, the most westerly of Andalucía's provinces, one of the most popular religious festivals in the region's Catholic calendar takes place annually at Pentecost, the fiftieth day after Easter. The Romería de El Rocío attracts thousands upon thousands of people to Almonte, a village of just over 1500 inhabitants.

Some years, the number of pilgrims making their way there to the shrine of the Virgen del Rocío has been known to reach nearly one million. The atmosphere, in a rural community suddenly swelled to four or five hundred times its size, is extraordinary.

The original shrine was constructed at the end of the 13th century in Las Rocinas on land re-conquered from the Moors by the Christians. It was destroyed as a result of the massive earthquake that hit nearby Portugal in 1755 and a larger sanctuary for the image of the Virgin was built five years later at Almonte. This was demolished in the mid-20th century and in 1969 the present one, with its two-tiered bell tower above a shell-shaped portico, was erected and blessed.

During the second and third weeks of May, at a time when patios are at their finest, full of flowers, ferns and shrubs, the city of Córdoba holds its Festival de los Patios. The patios, with their profusion of colours and shades of green, in pots, urns and hanging baskets, are tended with enormous care and, for these two weeks only, thrown open to the public.

The first records of this festival date back to 1918 but it was not until the early 1930s that it began to gain the popularity enjoyed to this day. More than 40 patios in the centre take part and entry is free of charge. Since the mid-1940s the festival has also included a competition with sought-after prizes, not so much for the money though, more for the prestige.

In the height of the summer, when hot air shimmers above parched fields all day, Andalucía comes to life at night. Much of the entertainment is held in the open air with shows and concerts usually not starting until well after sunset.

Purchena, a town in the province of Almería, has, since 1993, held its unique Juegos Moriscos, or Moorish Games. They revive a tradition started in the mid-16th century by Aben Humeya, one of the last Moorish leaders ruling under Felipe II of Spain.

Now declared a Fiesta of National Tourist Interest by the Junta de Andalucía, the 'games' include competitions of different sports based roughly on the Olympics. There are also musical and dance contests, with the added attractions of a *zoco*, or arts and crafts market, and live concerts of Arab and ethnic music in the evenings. This three-day event, which includes age-old contests of wrestling, archery and weight-lifting, takes place on the first weekend in August.

At the end of September, to mark the transition from summer to autumn and from the end of the harvest season to the beginning of another agrarian year, Úbeda holds its Feria de San Miguel. One of the oldest and most important festivals in the province of Jaén, it dates back to the early 13th century when Fernando III 'El Santo' re-conquered the town.

Nowadays, with a mixture of cultural and sporting activities, as well as pageantry and religion on the agenda, it includes orchestral concerts and padel-tennis competitions, bullfights and puppet theatres. And, in common with *ferias* held throughout Andalucía, it would not be complete without a daytime horticultural show and the vibrant, pulsing fairground at night.

Traditional chair restoration

Restoration and revival

Generations of *campesinos* may have built their country *casitas* over Phoenician factories, Roman baths or Arab houses. More recently, a developer, unaware of the treasures beneath his machines, might have bulldozed and buried priceless evidence of past civilisations. But today, Andalucía leads the way in matters of conservation and restoration.

In recognition of work carried out at the archaeological site of Medina Azahara, the culture department of the Junta de Andalucía received an award from the European Community. This lost Moorish city near Córdoba is where slaves once stirred a great bowl of mercury to amuse the caliph and a fish farm provided his court with daily fresh food. The site continues to reveal new insights into history and the way of life of those bygone days. Apart from restoring the ancient marble and limestone floors, one of the most important works to be carried out here has been the conservation of the imposing *ataurique* entrance door, with its fragile and intricate plaster decoration using plant motifs so typical of Moorish art.

Plans are also under way for the restoration of one of the most interesting examples of defensive architecture in the province of Jaén: the Alcázar de la Mota at Alcalá la Real. Constructed by the Moors in the 8th century on a 1000-metre high rocky outcrop, the castle was the scene of many confrontations between warring Muslim families.

During the Christian Reconquest of Al-Andalus this fortress complex was attacked successively by Alfonso VIII, Fernando II and Alfonso X, before passing finally into Spanish hands in 1341 during the reign of Alfonso XI. One day soon, much more of this triple-walled castle may be seen in all its former splendour.

Old paintings have been brought vividly back to life, primitive bronze statues have been conserved and insights into language usage and definition have been revived. Ancient dolmens, uncovered during excavation work on a highway, are on display in an Estepona museum built in the style of a prehistoric necropolis.

In the Plaza de Merced in Málaga, buildings have been refurbished. Their new façades are almost indistinguishable from the old, reviving the classic 18th-century architectural lines that can be seen elsewhere around the square.

Roman legionnaires are remembered for building straight roads across Andalucía. Not so well known is the fact that they brought with them, along those ancient highways, sackloads of their favourite food: chestnuts. Planting large estates of the best sweet-chestnut trees in Europe, they, and later the Moors, nurtured the forests and harvested abundant crops.

Descendants of those trees remain, but the old custom of farming the chestnuts declined over the centuries. In today's so-called organic age, the chestnut's natural goodness and versatility in healthy eating is once again being recognised. Near Aracena, in the northern part of the province of Huelva, local farmers are reviving this ancient agricultural activity and creating new plantations for future generations.

Dressed for the Verdiales

Villancicos and *zambombas*

From classical concerts and grand oratorios performed in small churches or large cathedrals, to groups of carollers singing on a street corner, music in December assumes a different mood from the rest of the year. Some music fiestas and festivals, whose origins can be traced to the ancient settlers of southern Spain, also take place around that time. If you take a moment out from the frenetic festivities to listen to the tunes and lyrics, you will be conveyed back in time to the compositions brought to Andalucía by other cultures.

Almost everywhere in the world, Christmas carols are an inseparable part of the seasonal festivities. Each country has its own tunes and lyrics, but perhaps the best known is *Noche de Paz*, or 'Silent Night', which has been translated into more than 300 different languages. The words were written in 1816 by Joseph Mohr, a priest in the Austrian village of Oberndorf.

Two years later, wanting to introduce a new carol at midnight mass, he took the verse to his organist friend, Franz Xavier Gruber, who composed the now internationally famous tune.

Legend has it that most of the organ pipes had been eaten away by the mice, so the lyrics were originally set to the guitar, an unusual instrument to be heard in a church at that time. The carol immediately became popular. It was taken up by families of travelling folk singers, heard by kings and emperors and, before the end of the 19th century, had spread throughout the rest of Europe and to Andalucía.

In Spain, the precursor of the carol is the *villancico*, one of the most ancient forms of popular lyrics in this country. Its origins can be traced to the 15th century when the first documented records appeared, written down by Juan del Encina. Although today the format of his compositions seems quite usual, at the time it was innovative, consisting of a musical and poetic form, in which short verses sung by a soloist alternated with a repetitive chorus sung by the whole group.

In the late-16th century these songs of courtly love took on the religious aspect now associated with them. The church authorities were beginning to realise that if the Spanish language, instead of Latin, were introduced into the liturgy then perhaps they could reach out to the masses and instil in them the mysteries of the Catholic faith. Composing religious carols at that time developed into a very necessary prerequisite for a choir master if he wanted to be sure of keeping his job. They became more technically complex, and records exist of music written not just for one soloist but for six or more, accompanied by the harp, violin, organ and, of course, the choir.

By the 19th century, as *villancicos* became more popular in Andalucía, they were infused little by little with flamenco rhythms and styles. Less complex in structure than pure flamenco, with a simple harmonic melody, they had and continue to have popular appeal throughout the region. The Centro Andaluz de Flamenco, based in Jerez de la Frontera, houses an extensive collection of data regarding this musical genre and also works hard at keeping the traditional music and lyrics alive by organising singing competitions and festivals.

Other musical traditions in Andalucía during the festive season are the *verdiales*, one of the earliest forms of fandango. In common with much of the culture here, they were possibly introduced into the area by the Moors around the 8th century. Some historians, however, say they are Roman in origin, or even take them back to ancient Greece. They first developed in the olive growing area to the north of Málaga known as Los Verdiales. This name comes from a particular type of olive called the *verdial*, a word that derives from the Latin for verdant, or green. In Spanish: *verde*.

The music of the *verdiales* is to be danced to, common throughout the centuries at weddings, first communions and other family celebrations especially in the villages. A dance for couples in small or large groups, it involves a lot of leaping up and down so can be fairly strenuous. The members of these *pandas*, as the groups are called, wear colourful costumes which they festoon with bells and beads, ribbons and even mirrors, and their multi-coloured headgear usually abounds with flowers.

The lyrics of the *verdiales*, normally quite simple and of a happy nature, are frequently and spontaneously punctuated by a loud cry of '*ay*' and the music, provided by *bandurrias* (a stringed instrument similar to a lute), tambourines and castanets, is regularly accompanied by the spirited clicking of fingers.

The *pandas de verdiales* can be seen in many towns throughout southern Andalucía during the summer when they hold their local fiestas. There are also festivals dedicated solely to the *verdiales* which take place mainly in the Montes de Málaga and the Axarquía region, or in the area of the Guadalhorce valley. But the principal celebration is the Fiesta Mayor de Verdiales, which is held on 28th December in the small town of Puerta de la Torre, near Almogía. A platform is set up where *pandas* from surrounding villages compete with each other, but the impromptu practice sessions taking place around the town probably provide a more authentic experience. They are certainly livelier, as bottles of Málaga wine, *anís* (aniseed) or *aguadiente* (fire water) are regularly passed from one participant to another.

The day before *Nochebuena*, or Christmas Eve, is the traditional time for a *zambomba*. The fiesta, taking its name from a rustic percussion instrument, has been one of the popular cultural traditions in Andalucía since the 18th century, especially in Jerez de la Frontera. Made by hand, the instrument comprises an earthenware vessel covered with animal skin, usually goat. A long piece of cane is inserted through the centre which, when dampened and rubbed between the hands, emits a deep, earthy sound that provides the rhythm for the songs.

Most other genres of festive music are non-participatory, that is, a group of musicians plays for the enjoyment of the crowd and there is a distinct separation between the players and the public. With the *zambomba*, however, everyone takes part.

In the *casas de vecinos* in Jerez de la Frontera, where the front doors of houses or apartments overlook a central courtyard, it is customary for everyone to gather there to sing and dance, drink wine and eat traditional festive food such as *buñuelos*, a type of sugary doughnut.

Other instruments played alongside the *zambomba* at the fiesta are the *almirez* (a mortar made of metal), *pandereta* (tambourine) and the distinctive *anís* glass bottle with its lines of bumps over which a piece of wood is passed back and forth: simple percussion instruments. Everyone joins in, either clapping hands (*palmas*) or stamping feet (*zapateado*), knocking a spoon against their glass or a wooden spatula against a saucepan. Spontaneous singing is welcomed. A *copla*, or verse, sung by one person is taken up by the rest in joyful homage to the spirit of Christmas and to the seasonal festivities that mark the end of the year.

Almonds sellers in Málaga

Seasonal confectionery

Modern society in Andalucía is as much a melting pot as ever. Different customs touch and merge and the weeks from the end of November into January present a festive time for almost everyone. Children in many northern European countries eagerly await the arrival on 6th December of Saint Nicholas, who will bring them a gift or two. Spanish children have to be patient for another month, until 6th January, when the *Reyes Magos* or Three Kings come to town. But in between there is Christmas, with Santa Claus, Father Christmas, or Papa Noël; celebrated by the Spanish and the majority of other Europeans, on the evening of the 24th, *Nochebuena*.

As the lights are strung across the streets and decorations glitter in the windows, marzipan, one of the seasonal delights, appears in the shops. According to Italian legend, marzipan originated in Venice in the 16th century as *pan de San Marcos,* or bread of Saint Mark, in honour of the city's patron saint. Created out of ground almonds and sugar, it was a substitute 'bread' for the poor and hungry who could not afford that made from wheat or other cereals. But it is also recorded that the Greeks in the 4th century BC delighted in eating a round, flat 'cake' composed of almonds and honey.

Toledo too has its tales to tell. When the Spanish city was re-conquered in 1085 by Alfonso VI, after being settled by the Moors for two centuries, the monks of the Convento de San Clemente made *mazapán* to celebrate the victory. It is now produced in all shapes, sizes and colours, but for the most part only seen in the shops towards the end of the year, along with crystallised fruits.

The festive season is definitely a time for setting aside the diets and indulging in some Spanish confectionery at its best – *polvorones* and *mantecados*, *turrones* and *roscones*.

The secret of enjoying *polvorones* is to squeeze them tightly before unwrapping. A very *andaluz* tradition, these mouth-watering treats will scatter *polvo*, or powder, all over you if not compacted. They are chiefly made in Antequera and Estepa and originate from the traditional family celebration of the *matanza*, the pre-Christmas killing of the pig.

The animal, cared for almost like a pet throughout the year, was, and still is in some country areas, slaughtered at this time to provide food and plenty of *manteca*, or pork fat, for the coming hard months of winter. Every part of the pig is used and one by-product the *mantecados* which are made with flour, pork fat and sugar.

One of the first documented records in Spain of *turrón* appeared at the beginning of the 17th century, describing how it was made in the town of Jijona, near Alicante. Similar to French *nougat*, it consists of toasted almonds, ground or chopped, which are combined with *piñones* (pine nuts), *avellanas* (hazel nuts) or *nueces* (walnuts) and mixed with honey or sugar. Jijona remains to this day the centre of Spanish *turrón* manufacture. The original recipe has been varied and it is now also made with coconut, which arrived in Spain in the 18th century, and more recently with chocolate or various fruits.

The crowning glory of the *Fiestas de Navidad* is the *Roscón de Reyes*, a large, ring-shaped confection eaten on the 6th January. Its pagan origin goes back to Roman times when the New Year fell on the first day of March and the *roscón*, or ring, represented the beginning of a new seasonal cycle.

The Romans took their traditions with them when they conquered Gaul, as we know from the famous Asterix series, and there the custom was 'Christianised'. Eventually finding its way south to Spain, the *roscón* now symbolises the crown of one of the Three Kings and is topped with 'jewels' of crystallised fruits.

A relatively new tradition in Spanish culture is that of the *doce uvas*, the twelve grapes. It is said to date from the over-abundant harvest of 1909 which produced too much fruit to eat, turn into wine or convert into raisins. Unwilling to let them rot, or to throw away the produce of their hard work over the year, farmers apparently came up with the idea that if each person in the country ate twelve grapes on New Year's Eve, *Nochevieja*, then this would help solve the problem. Since then millions have been consumed on the last day of the year.

Though now sold in small tins, already peeled and de-pipped, the custom used to be for the youngest member of the family to prepare the pile of twelve for everyone around the family's festive table. One grape to be eaten on each stroke of midnight to welcome in the *Año Nuevo*, one grape for luck in each month of the New Year. Good luck for everyone. *¡Suerte para todos!*

GLOSSARY OF SPANISH WORDS

Español	**English**
acequia	irrigation ditch
aceituna	olive
acueducto	aqueduct
aguardiente	firewater (pure alcohol)
alarife	head of construction works
alberca	water deposit
alcazaba	Moorish citadel
alcázar	Moorish fortress
algarrobo	carob tree
andaluz	person from Andalucía
anís	aniseed
arrayanes	myrtle bushes
arte rupestre	cave painting / rock art
aulaga morisca	gorse-like shrub with yellow flowers
avellana	hazel nut
ataurique	plaster decoration depicting plant life
baile	dance
bandurria	stringed instrument similar to lute
bóveda	vault
breva	fig (first crop)
buñuelo	type of sugary doughnut
cajón	box (used as percussion instrument)
caló	gypsy dialect
campesino/a	country dweller
campo	countryside
cangilones	buckets on waterwheel
cantaor/a	flamenco singer
cante	singing
cante jondo	traditional flamenco singing
casita	small house in country
castaña	chestnut
castillo	castle
chirigota	satirical song, popular at Cádiz carnival
compás	musical measure / rhythm
copla	sung verse
costalero/a	man / woman bearing Easter Week image

cueva	cave
Denominación de Origen	Protected Designation of Origin
dólmen	dolmen
Domingo de Ramos	Palm Sunday
Domingo de la Resurrección	Easter Sunday
duende	spirit/magic/mystery/soul
farruca	type of flamenco song
finca	country property
fortaleza	stronghold
fuente	fountain
gaditano/a	person from Cádiz
gitano/a	gypsy
grafitero/a	graffiti artist
granada	pomegranate
higo	fig (second crop)
iglesia	church
ingenio	sugar refinery
jerezano/a	person from Jerez de la Frontera
malagueño/a	person from Málaga
mantecado	confectionery made with pork fat
meseta	plateau
miliario	roadside stone marking 1000 paces
mozárabe	Mozarab (Christian under Moorish rule)
mudéjar	style of Moorish/Christian architecture
nevero	man who collected snow
Nochebuena	Christmas Eve
Nochevieja	New Year's Eve
noria	waterwheel
nueces	walnuts
olivo	olive tree
palmas	clapping with the hands
palo flamenco	musical style of flamenco
pandereta	tambourine
peña flamenca	association of flamenco enthusiasts
piñones	pine nuts
plata	silver
polvorones	confectionery of flour, pork fat and sugar
pozo de nieve	snow well

reconquista	Christian re-conquest of Moorish Spain
Reyes Magos	Three Kings
roscón de Reyes	ring-shaped cake baked for Epiphany
ruta	route
saeta	type of flamenco song
Semana Santa	Easter week
sevillana	type of flamenco dance
sevillano/a	person from Sevilla
tablao	club where flamenco is performed
toque	guitar playing in flamenco music
torre	tower
turrón	sweet made with almonds and honey
verdiales	festive music typical of Málaga province
vía verde	green route
villancico	carol sung at Christmas time
zambomba	traditional percussion instrument
zapateado	foot stamping in flamenco dance